# DINING IN

## G. GARVIN

MEREDITH® BOOKS • DES MOINES, IOWA

Meredith Books

Meredith Books
1716 Locust Street
Des Moines, Iowa 50309-3023
meredithbooks.com

Printed in the United States of America.
First Edition.
Library of Congress Control Number: 2008924201
ISBN: 978-0-696-23831-4



Cover photography and images of G. Garvin: Whitney Thomas

**dedication** I dedicate this book to my beautiful daughter. When I can't find the words to write, I simply listen to the words in your heart. As I look at you and see so much of myself, I read the words in your smile. When I can't get the recipe to work after trying it time and time again, you look at me and say, "Daddy, like you always tell me, you can't quit." So there I stand doing and doing until I get it right. It is truly just the thought of my child that gives me the inspiration to do better—be better—so that she might one day do and think the same. As I have said before to my greatest accomplishment, delivered by hand from God, I thank and dedicate this book to you, my sweet child, Nola Miles Mihaly Garvin. I love you with not just all of my heart but with all of my soul. Love, Dad.

“MOST OF THE TIME IT’S EASY TO TALK ABOUT WHAT’S NOT GOOD IN OUR LIVES. SO I ASK YOU TO TAKE A FEW MOMENTS TO THINK ABOUT THE THINGS THAT ARE POSTIVE IN YOUR LIFE. AND SIT BACK AND ENJOY WHAT YOU ARE THANKFUL FOR.

—G”

**thank you** My man Whitney Thomas for his great cover work. Charlie Mack for his insight on the connection of Whitney and me. Shawn Porter of 215 Exclusive Salon for always keeping me Philly fresh. My great team at Power House Productions for its never-ending support and much valued insight. TV One for its support on all three books and many purchases for the TV One family. Lynn McReynolds for always being there in a PR way. Carol H. Williams Advertising Agency for their trust and dedication to G. Garvin. To Marc Brogden from N2U Creative Marketing Group, thanks for all you do and the role you played in the success of the first two books. AGMB Law and staff, thank you. My dear friend, Marsha Carter, thanks for your great help on this book and always being there when I'm in need of any—and all things—food. The big homie, Dennis Ellis: thank you for sharing such a special recipe from such a very special person in your life. Buddy Triadad, yo B, thank you so much for all of your dessert work on this book. For years we have worked so closely and this was a true pleasure for me. Thank you. LaDonna Hughley, Sauna Vaughn, and Pamela Chestnut for being such great friends. The three of you are like sisters from another mother. Thank you for being there.

Hoyett Owens and Faith Morris of Owens Morris Communications, thank you for trusting me to lead so many great opportunities on your behalf. Pastor Barry and Kimberly and the entire Living Water church family for finally giving me a permanent church to call home.

To Mom and my sisters, you know your names by now— I hope.

I love and thank every person on this page because so much of my success is due to your continuous hard work and dedication to the development of G. Garvin.

# contents

## introduction

As I finish my third book—something I'm so very excited about and also super thankful for—I realize that writing a book is much like making a dinner party.

So much happens between the time a book is just an idea and when it is in your hands. Maybe you're reading this while you're standing at the bookstore in the cookbook section or maybe you're turning the pages for the first time at home. This moment you're having right now is what inspired me to make this book.

The thought and care that go into food and dinner parties is similar because your guests never see the beginning steps or the challenges along the way. They just show up to this beautiful room and wonderful-smelling kitchen. Well, this book is going to show you how to dine in with your family and friends—the simple way, of course.

Now, I know there are all types of cooks. Some are always coming up with new and fresh ideas for the next meal. Some get a little nervous but keep going. And some just panic, afraid to try anything new. Well, you can all relax now because ***Dining In*** is your informal guide to taking simple recipes and ideas and giving them a gourmet twist. These dishes use familiar ingredients—with a few tricks. I'll show you how to turn your next dinner party into a dining experience with my surprisingly easy presentation and set-up ideas.

My goal is to help you challenge yourself to try something new—without the worry of failure. So thank you for trusting me while you and I dig a little deeper to tap into your creativity and imagination through your love for food, family, and fun.

These days I find myself cooking and entertaining more for smaller, private events or for close friends and family. And I find that everyone (myself included) is becoming interested in more than just cooking the meal—it's also about the shopping, the dining room, and the table setting. I even find myself enjoying shopping for the fresh flowers for the house and putting them together before I start to cook.

Dining in is something that everyone can enjoy—weekend cooks, experienced cooks, even beginner cooks. It's a lot simpler than you would think. But people still assume that dining in is difficult because they don't have anyone to ask for advice. Well, you've got me and this book. A great evening is possible if you decide that it's something you're willing to try.

It all starts with having fun with the food—old and new, easy and more challenging. Start with recipes you're comfortable with and throw in some newer ones. Kick up that easy recipe with an awesome presentation. I say for every three old ideas, try to introduce one new one (such as the dishes in this book).

Remember that different does not have to mean difficult—and difficult certainly doesn't mean a dish is different or better.

As you begin putting together your shopping list, include other things on your to-do list. Dining in is about setting the tone. So get your guests involved in preparing the room and setting the table while you pour a few glasses of your favorite wine. Break out the greatest hits from Prince, James Brown, Marvin Gaye, or (one of my personal favorites) Frankie Beverly and Maze. When I get friends and family involved, dining in becomes not just dinner at G. Garvin's house but a wonderful experience with family and friends at G. Garvin's house.

I want to get back to spending the right amount of time on dinner, and by that I mean taking the time to think it all through. I promise you this: If you spend more time putting it together, your guests will enjoy it more and be more thankful for what you have done—which in the end will translate into a wonderful evening.

I think back to the days when I was a little boy celebrating Easter Sunday at New Hope Church in Atlanta. All the adults—my mom, Eleanor; Gwen; Lula; Mary; Miss Ruenette; Uncle Moses—spent all Saturday night cooking at home and in the church kitchen. And you best believe they could cook! The older boys cut the grass on Saturday, while the older girls picked fresh flowers for the tables. Those Easter dinners were almost like dinner parties. We ate downstairs in the basement of the church, but the room was beautiful. The tables were set with polished antique silver borrowed from all the aunties and grandmas in the neighborhood. The smell of the food was strong and friendly—fried chicken, steak and onions, sugar snap peas, hot water corn bread, good old mac and cheese. There were no strangers: If you were in the house of New Hope on Easter, then you were the family of New Hope.

Likewise, the most important thing about dining in is taking the time to show people who are important to you that you enjoy sharing your heavenly trinity—your home, your heart, and your food. Trust me, dining in is not complicated; if it's in your heart, then it's so easy. (And if I can do it, then so can you!)

Enjoy!

“IT ALL STARTS WITH HAVING FUN WITH THE FOOD—OLD AND NEW, EASY AND MORE CHALLENGING.

—G”

## wine pairing

When you walk into a wine shop it's easy to get intimidated by all those choices—especially when you're trying to pick out something to go with a specific dish. Relax! Here are a few reds and whites I enjoy, along with recipes to pair with them:

### WHITE WINES

**MERK PINOT GRIGIO (2004)**
*Friuli, Italy*
- Calamari-Rock Shrimp Salad with Frisée, page 116
- Sautéed Calamari with Cherry Tomatoes, Black Mussels, and Clams, page 117

**LEDGEWOOD CREEK SAUVIGNON BLANC (2006)**
*Suisun Valley, California*
- Chicken Breasts Stuffed with Goat Cheese, Basil, and Sun-dried Tomatoes, page 49
- Grilled Swordfish with Sautéed Bay Shrimp and Crab, page 107

**DI LENARDO VINEYARDS PINOT GRIGIO (2006)**
*Venezia Giulia, Italy*
- Poached Red Snapper with Avocado, White Peach, and Cilantro Salsa, page 93
- Pan-Roasted Breast of Chicken with Morels and Arugula, page 52

**VIA AGUA FRESCA SAUVIGNON BLANC (2006)**
*Casablanca Valley, Chile*
- Pan-Seared Chilean Sea Bass with Crispy Onions and Chive Beurre Blanc, page 96
- Steamed Black Mussels with Garlic and Cream, page 83
- Cast Iron-Roasted Seafood Sizzle with Lemon, page 111

**ROBLEDO SEVEN BROTHERS SAUVIGNON BLANC (2006)**
*Lake County, California*
- 5-Spice-Marinated Herbed Chicken, page 152
- Baked Alaskan Halibut with Fresh Herbs and Roasted Red Bee Potatoes, page 105

### RED WINES

**MILL CREEK VINEYARDS ESTATE MERLOT (2002)**
*Dry Creek Valley, Sonoma County, California*
- Seasoned Filet Mignon with Whole Garlic, page 143
- Slow-Roasted Lamb Shanks, page 68
- Pan-Roasted New York Steak with Onions and Warm Spinach, page 72

**FRANCIS COPPOLA DIAMOND SERIES CALIFORNIA MERLOT (2005)**
*Rutherford, California*
- Marinated T-bone Steak, page 139
- Grilled Black Pepper and Sea Salt-Crusted Cowboy Ribeye Steak, page 142

**MONTICELLO VINEYARDS ESTATE GROWN PINOT NOIR (2004)**
*Oak Knoll District, Napa Valley, California*
- Prosciutto-Wrapped Pork Tenderloin with Braised Mushroom Ragoût, page 124
- Pan-Fried Medallions of Venison with Black Truffle Mashed Potatoes, Trumpet Mushrooms, and Warm Bacon Reduction, page 75
- Braised Cornish Game Hen with Potatoes and Leeks, page 131

**FINCA EL RETIRO SYRAH (2004)**
*Mendoza, Argentina*
- Braised Veal Loin with Trumpet Mushrooms, page 130
- Grilled Boneless Leg of Lamb, page 70
- Braised Short Rib Stew with Truffle Rice, page 126

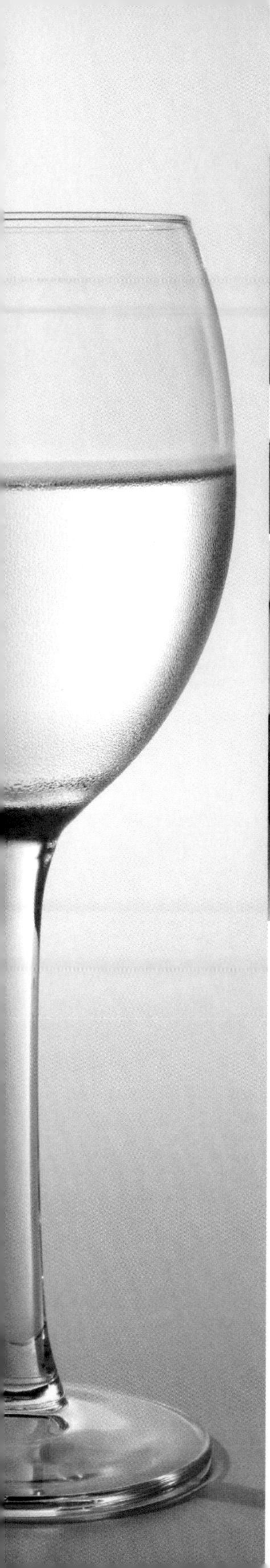

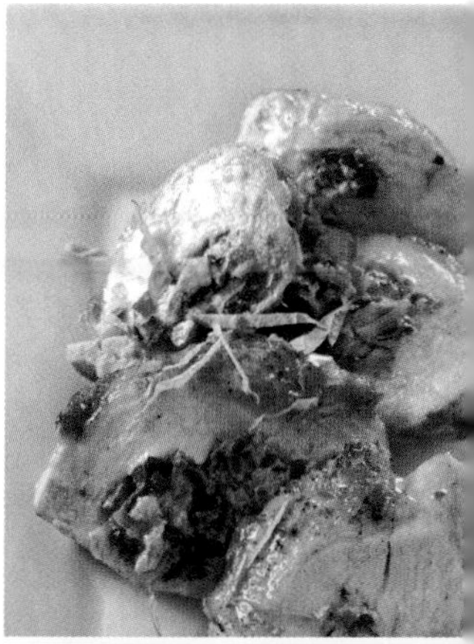

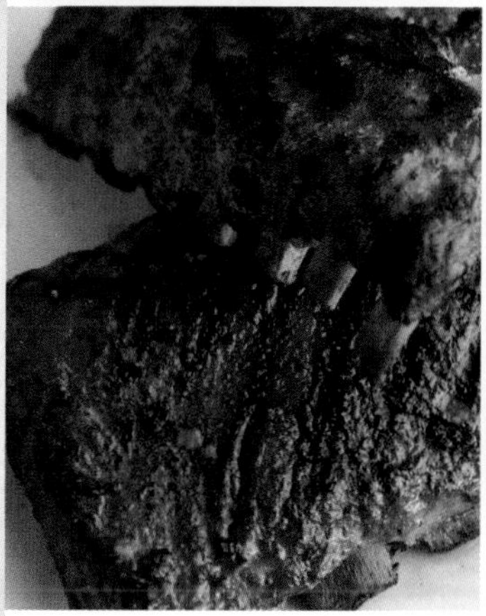

## SAKE

When buying sake, you need to go with a high-end brand. Inexpensive sake—say, less than $15 or $20 for a full-size (720-750 ml) bottle—won't let you experience the smoothness and bold, clean flavor this beverage is all about. And there's no way to cut corners on this because making really good sake is never cheap for the producer. They actually have to mill away a big portion of each and every grain of rice in order to get rid of impurities that can cause off flavors.

There are lots of different styles of sake, and I pick one based on the type of fish or meat I'm serving. I do tend to stick with lighter varieties and serve them chilled. Just like learning about wine or cigars, learning about sake never stops, so take good notes every time you try a new one.

# set the tone

LIKE GREAT FOOD, MUSIC HAS THE POWER TO MOVE YOU EMOTIONALLY. SO LOAD UP THE PLAYER WITH SOME OF YOUR FAVORITES TO HELP CREATE THE RIGHT MOOD FOR THE EVENING. HERE'S A FEW OF MINE.

MUSIQ
COLE
just like you
BEST OF
gaye
disc one
UTVRECORDS
440 014 368-2 [440 014 367-2]

## show it off

Here you see four little tricks of the trade that, once you try 'em, you'll find yourself using a lot. All very easy. All go-to techniques. So let's talk presentation first, because we want to really pop that food off the plate visually, creating a treat for the eyes that sets up the incredible flavor that's on its way.

### BALSAMIC REDUCTION (see photo 1)

Just an easy syrup you simmer on the stove—does this in a big, big way. Drizzling tangy-sweet streaks on the plate creates an awesome base for the food.

**2 cups balsamic vinegar**
**½ cup brown sugar**
**½ cup red wine**

Stir together all ingredients in a pot and bring to a simmer. Simmer until a spoon inserted into the liquid holds an even coating on the back when removed.

### GREEN OIL (see photo 2)

A big part of this is the gorgeous color, which adds a cool, fresh feel to an entrée. All it takes is just a few tiny, bright drops and pools here and there to really bring a dish to life. Go for it!

**1 cup extra virgin olive oil**
**1 bunch parsley**
**1 cup fresh baby spinach**
**Pinch kosher salt**

Place all ingredients in a food processor and pulse until well blended. Strain mixture through a very fine strainer or cheese cloth.

### USING A RING MOLD (see photo 3)

Now here I'm using a 4-inch ring mold to form and hold together layers of crab and avocado. Not only is this tool ideal for presenting salads and seafood like these, it'll work with all kinds of small grains as well as finely chopped tomatoes and other vegetables. Do you need to go out searching for a ring mold? Probably not—if you have a biscuit cutter you're already in business. It works almost as well.

### SHAVING GARLIC (see photo 4)

Finally, I want to explain something I call for in many of the recipes—shaved garlic. OK, by shaved I don't mean that you need to break out a razor blade. But you do want to use a very sharp chef's knife and carefully slice off extremely thin pieces lengthwise (take another look at that photo!) from each clove. The size and shape isn't only important for flavor but for appearance and texture as well. And there you have it!

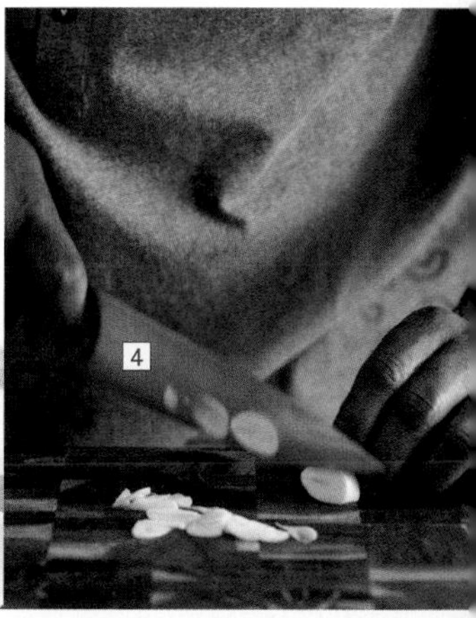

## basic recipes

Every cook needs a few tried and true side dish recipes—sides that'll back up lots of different entrées with satisfying flavors everyone knows and loves. When you're building a great dish, these are my go-to favorites.

### GARLIC MASHED POTATOES

makes 4 servings

- 1 bulb garlic
- Olive oil
- 6 white rose potatoes, peeled and quartered
- 2 tablespoons unsalted butter
- 1 cup heavy cream

1. Preheat oven to 375°F. Cut garlic bulb in half to expose the cloves. Drizzle with olive oil. Wrap in foil and bake for 20 to 25 minutes or until garlic is tender. Cool. Squeeze the cloves from the bulb, discarding any outer peel from roasted cloves.

2. Meanwhile place a large pot of water on the stove; add potatoes. Bring to boiling. Reduce heat and simmer for 15 to 20 minutes or until tender. Drain and set aside.

3. In a medium saucepan, melt the butter over medium heat. Add cream and bring to a simmer. Add the roasted garlic cloves. Mash the potatoes. Slowly add the hot cream mixture to the potatoes; whip to desired consistency. Season with salt and pepper.

### PARMESAN AND CHEDDAR CHEESE GRITS

makes 4 servings

- 4 cups water
- 1/2 teaspoon salt
- 1 cup uncooked fine or medium hominy grits
- 1/2 cup shredded cheddar cheese
- 1/2 cup shredded Parmesan cheese
- 1 tablespoon unsalted butter
- Ground black pepper

1. In a small saucepan bring the water and salt to a boil. Whisk in the grits and continue to whisk for about 1 minute. When the mixture returns to boiling, reduce heat to low. Cook for 10 to 15 minutes or until creamy and smooth, stirring frequently.

2. Remove from heat. Stir in cheeses, butter, and pepper to taste.

### SAFFRON SUN-DRIED TOMATO RISOTTO

makes 4 servings

- 5 to 6 cups chicken broth
- 1 cup chopped onion
- 5 tablespoons olive oil
- 1 cup Arborio rice
- 1 tablespoon chopped garlic
- Small pinch saffron threads
- 1/2 cup sun-dried tomatoes (oil-packed), coarsely chopped
- 3 tablespoons shredded Parmesan cheese
- 1 tablespoon butter, melted
- 2 teaspoons salt
- 2 teaspoons ground black pepper

1. In a medium pot bring broth to boiling; reduce heat to a simmer. In a medium saucepan sauté 1/2 cup of the onion in 1 tablespoon of the olive oil over medium heat, stirring until the onion is tender but not brown. Add the rice, garlic, and saffron; stir to combine.

2. Increase heat to medium-high. Stir in 1/2 cup of the hot broth; simmer, stirring constantly. As the broth is absorbed, continue to add broth, 1/2 cup at a time, while stirring constantly. Cook until rice is three-quarters of the way done (just starting to get tender). Remove from heat.

3. In a second pot heat the remaining 4 tablespoons olive oil over low heat. Add the remaining 1/2 cup onion and sauté until tender. Add the partially cooked risotto and 1/4 cup of the broth; cook and stir constantly until desired consistency is reached. Stir in tomatoes, Parmesan cheese, melted butter, salt, and pepper.

### JASMINE RICE

makes 3 1/2 cups

- 1 1/2 cups jasmine rice
- 1 3/4 cups cold water
- 1 tablespoon chopped fresh Italian (flat-leaf) parsley
- Kosher salt

1. Rinse the rice until water runs clear. Drain. Place rice and cold water in a large saucepan. Bring to boiling. Reduce heat and simmer, covered, for 20 minutes or until rice is tender. Remove from heat; let stand for 10 minutes.

2. Fluff rice with a fork; add parsley. Toss with a fork to combine. Season with salt to taste.

# 1
# ALL THINGS PASTA

**what I love** about a great pasta is that you can do so much with it. Penne. Rigatoni. Pappardelle. Capellini. They are all such great shapes to build a meal around. And an insanely good pasta sauce for your family or a table full of guests is truly simple to do. Just combine crushed tomatoes, smashed garlic, fresh mushrooms, and a few shallots along with some wine, butter, and herbs. And don't forget the freshly grated Parmesan cheese. This chapter offers a few easy recipes for cooking up this kitchen staple.

# linguine and ground beef with tomato and prosciutto

makes 4 servings

- 1 pound dried linguine
- 1/2 pound ground beef
- 2 tablespoons shaved garlic
- Kosher salt and ground black pepper
- 2 cups red cherry tomatoes, halved
- 1 cup chicken stock or broth
- 6 slices prosciutto
- 2 tablespoons unsalted butter
- 1/4 cup finely shredded Parmesan cheese

1. Preheat oven to 400°F. Cook pasta according to package directions.

2. While the pasta is cooking, place the ground beef and garlic in a large saucepan over medium heat; season with salt and pepper. Cook until brown, about 5 minutes; drain fat. Add the tomatoes and the chicken stock. Bring to boiling. Reduce heat and simmer, uncovered, for 5 to 7 minutes.

3. While the sauce is cooking, place the prosciutto on a baking sheet and bake for 4 to 6 minutes or until fat is golden and meat darkens.

4. Stir the butter into the sauce. Add the drained cooked pasta; toss well to combine. Add the cheese. Spoon the pasta into single-size servings, roughly break the prosciutto over the top, and serve.

# fusilli with ground beef, sun-dried tomatoes, and sautéed onions

makes 4 servings

- 1 pound dried fusilli pasta
- 1/2 pound ground beef (chuck)
- 1 small Spanish onion or other sweet yellow onion, diced
- 1 teaspoon shaved garlic
- 1 cup white wine
- 1/3 cup port wine
- 1 cup oil-packed sun-dried tomatoes, drained
- 2 tablespoons butter
- Kosher salt and ground black pepper

1. Cook the pasta according to package directions.

2. While the pasta is cooking, in a large sauté pan cook beef, onion, and garlic until meat is brown and onion is tender; drain fat. Add both the wines. Bring to boiling. Reduce heat and simmer, uncovered, for 3 minutes.

3. Add the drained cooked pasta and the sun-dried tomatoes; mix well. Fold in the butter. Season to taste with salt and pepper.

“STEP BACK WHEN YOU SERVE THIS DISH BECAUSE THE TASTE MIGHT MAKE YOUR GUESTS GO A LITTLE CRAZY.”

# penne with sautéed beef tenderloin, spinach, goat cheese, and plum tomatoes

makes 4 servings

- 1 pound dried penne pasta
- 1 tablespoon olive oil
- 2 tablespoons chopped shallots
- 1 tablespoon minced garlic
- 12 ounces beef tenderloin, cut in 1-inch pieces
- 2 cups white wine
- 2 cups canned Italian-style whole peeled tomatoes in puree
- 4 ounces goat cheese
- 2 tablespoons unsalted butter
- 9 ounces fresh spinach

1. Cook pasta according to package directions.

2. In a Dutch oven heat the oil over medium high heat. Add the shallots and garlic; sauté for 2 minutes. Add the beef tenderloin; sauté for another 2 minutes. Add the white wine and tomatoes. Bring to boiling. Reduce heat and simmer for 2 minutes.

3. Add the drained cooked pasta, goat cheese, and butter. Add spinach; stir until just wilted.

“THIS PASTA WILL FOR SURE TWEAK YOUR TASTEBUDS AND FILL YOU UP AT THE SAME TIME.”

# roasted short ribs

makes 4 servings

- 2 pounds beef short ribs
- 1 tablespoon kosher salt
- 1 tablespoon garlic salt
- 1 tablespoon onion powder
- 1 tablespoon seasoned salt
- 1 tablespoon finely ground black pepper
- 1 cup all-purpose flour
- 1/4 cup olive oil
- 2 large onions, chopped
- 1/4 cup chopped garlic
- 1/4 cup chopped shallots
- 3 sprigs rosemary
- Olive oil
- 2 cups white wine
- 2 cups chicken stock
- 1 cup water

1. Preheat oven to 350°F. Trim fat from around the short ribs. Rinse ribs in cool water and season with kosher salt, garlic salt, onion powder, seasoned salt, and pepper. Pat the seasonings in so they stick to the ribs. Set aside. Place flour on a large plate; set aside.

2. In a large roasting pan heat the 1/4 cup oil over medium heat. Dip one side of a short rib into the flour. Place rib in hot pan, floured side down. Repeat until all ribs are floured and are in pan. Cook until ribs are golden; turn ribs over.

3. Add the onions, garlic, and shallots and mix well. Add the rosemary and a splash of olive oil; mix well again. Add white wine, chicken stock, and water. Bring to a simmer.

4. Place a piece of foil over the roasting pan. Place pan in the oven for 1½ to 2 hours or until ribs are tender. (More time may be needed for very large ribs.)

**NOTE:** YOU MAY THINK IT IS STRANGE TO HAVE A SHORTRIB RECIPE IN THE PASTA SECTION. IT IS ESSENTIAL FOR THE INCREDIBLE PAPPARDELLE WITH ROASTED SHORTRIB RAGOÛT ON THE FOLLOWING PAGE.

# pappardelle with roasted short rib ragoût

makes 4 servings

- 1 recipe Roasted Short Ribs (see recipe, page 27)
- 1 pound dried pappardelle pasta
- 1 tablespoon olive oil
- 1/2 cup unsalted butter
- 3 tablespoons chopped shallots
- 2 cups canned Italian-style whole peeled tomatoes in puree, drained and cut up
- 1 teaspoon chopped fresh rosemary
- 1 teaspoon chopped fresh thyme
- 1 cup white wine
- Kosher salt and ground black pepper
- 1/4 cup finely shredded Parmesan cheese

1. Prepare the Roasted Short Ribs. Pull the short rib meat apart into shreds.

2. Cook pasta according to package directions.

3. For the ragoût, in a large saucepan heat oil and 1 tablespoon of the butter over medium heat. Add the short rib meat and the shallots; sauté for 3 minutes. Add the tomatoes, rosemary, and thyme. Stir in the white wine. Bring to boiling. Reduce heat and simmer, uncovered, for 10 minutes or until most of the liquid has evaporated. Fold in the remaining butter and season to taste with salt and pepper.

4. Add the drained cooked pasta and cheese to the sauce; toss to combine.

# pappardelle with chicken, pork, and veal sausage with fresh tomato

makes 4 servings

- 1 pound dried pappardelle pasta
- 1 tablespoon olive oil
- 1 tablespoon minced fresh garlic
- 2 cooked pork sausage links, coarsely chopped
- 2 cooked veal sausage links, coarsely chopped
- 2 cooked chicken sausage links, coarsely chopped
- 2 large vine-ripened tomatoes, coarsely chopped
- Kosher salt and ground black pepper
- 2 cups veal or chicken stock or broth
- 1 bunch fresh basil, chopped
- 1/4 cup finely shredded Parmesan cheese
- 2 tablespoons unsalted butter

1. Cook pasta according to package directions.

2. While the pasta is cooking, heat the oil in a large heavy bottomed saucepan. Add the garlic and sauté for 2 minutes. Add the sausages and tomatoes; season with salt and pepper. Add the stock. Bring to boiling. Reduce heat and simmer, uncovered, for 10 minutes.

3. Add the drained cooked pasta, the basil, cheese, and butter; mix well.

**NOTE:** SUBSTITUTE OTHER TYPES OF SAUSAGE IF YOU LIKE; JUST USE A TOTAL OF 6 LINKS.

# rigatoni with pork sausage, plum tomatoes, and sautéed onions

makes 4 servings

- 1 pound dried rigatoni pasta
- 1/2 pound pork sausage
- 1 onion, chopped
- 2 tablespoons shaved garlic
- 2 cups canned Italian-style whole peeled plum tomatoes, cut up
- 2 cups chicken stock or broth
- 1/2 cup coarsely chopped oil-packed sun-dried tomatoes, drained
- 1 teaspoon crushed red pepper
- Kosher salt and ground black pepper
- 2 tablespoons unsalted butter
- 1/4 cup finely shredded Parmesan cheese

1. Cook pasta according to package directions.

2. In a Dutch oven, cook sausage, onion, and garlic over medium-high heat until sausage is brown and onion is tender; drain fat. Add the tomatoes, chicken stock, sun-dried tomatoes, and crushed red pepper. Bring to boiling. Reduce heat and simmer, uncovered, for 5 minutes or to desired consistency. Season to taste with salt and pepper.

3. Add the drained cooked pasta, the butter, and the cheese.

# bbq chicken linguine, my oscar dish

makes 4 servings

- 1 pound dried linguine pasta
- 1 tablespoon olive oil
- 1 tablespoon diced shallots
- 1 teaspoon diced jalapeño chile pepper
- 12 ounces skinless boneless chicken thighs, chopped
- 1/4 cup chicken stock or broth
- 3/4 cup Bull's-Eye® or homemade barbecue sauce
- Grilled Asparagus (see recipe, below)

1. Cook the pasta according to package directions.

2. While the pasta is cooking, heat the oil in a medium sauté pan over medium heat. Add shallots and jalapeño pepper; sauté for 2 minutes. Add the chicken; sauté for 3 to 4 minutes or until chicken is no longer pink.

3. Add the drained cooked pasta, the stock, and half of the barbecue sauce; simmer for 2 minutes then add the remaining barbecue sauce. Serve with Grilled Asparagus.

GRILLED ASPARAGUS

Lightly coat a grill pan with olive oil. Remove tough stems from one bunch (about 1 pound) asparagus. Cut stalks into 2-inch pieces. Drizzle with 1 tablespoon olive oil; season with salt and pepper. Grill for 4 to 6 minutes in grill pan or until asparagus is tender.

“WHILE SERVING THIS PASTA TELL YOUR FRIENDS, 'ANYTIME, ANYWHERE, GET SOME OF THIS, 'CAUSE THIS IS HOW I GET DOWN.'”

# farfalle with ricotta, fresh spinach, sautéed chicken, and plum tomatoes

makes 4 servings

- 1 pound dried farfalle (bow tie) pasta
- 1 tablespoon olive oil
- 1 tablespoon shaved garlic
- 1 tablespoon chopped shallots
- 8 ounces cooked dark meat chicken, coarsely shredded
- 1 cup white wine
- 1 cup canned whole peeled tomatoes, drained and crushed
- 1 cup fresh spinach
- 1/4 cup ricotta cheese
- 1/4 cup heavy cream
- Kosher salt and ground black pepper
- Shaved Parmesan cheese (optional)

1. Cook the pasta according to package directions.

2. While the pasta is cooking, heat the oil in a medium sauté pan over medium heat. Once the oil is hot, add the garlic and shallot; sauté for 2 minutes. Add the chicken, white wine, and tomatoes; simmer for 2 minutes.

3. Add the drained cooked pasta, the spinach, the ricotta cheese, and the cream. Season to taste with salt and pepper. If desired, garnish with shaved Parmesan cheese.

**NOTE:** TRY USING THE DARK MEAT FROM A PURCHASED ROASTED CHICKEN FOR THIS DISH.

# angel hair pasta with sautéed lobster

makes 4 servings

1 pound dried angel hair pasta
1 3-pound lobster, cooked
1 tablespoon olive oil
2 tablespoons shaved garlic
1 cup white wine
2 tablespoons unsalted butter (optional)
1 teaspoon sugar
Kosher salt and ground black pepper

1. Cook pasta according to package directions.

2. While the pasta is cooking remove lobster meat from the shell and coarsely chop.

3. In a sauté pan heat the oil over medium heat. Add the garlic; sauté for 1 minute. Add the lobster and wine. Bring to boiling. Reduce heat and simmer, uncovered, for 3 minutes more. Add the butter, if desired, and the sugar.

4. Add the drained cooked pasta; mix well. Season to taste with salt and pepper.

# seafood pappardelle with dover sole

makes 4 servings

- 1 pound dried pappardelle pasta
- 1 tablespoon olive oil
- 16 ounces skinless sole fillets (Dover or other variety of sole)
- Kosher salt and ground black pepper
- 2 cups plum tomatoes, peeled and crushed
- 2 tablespoons shaved garlic
- 2 cups white wine
- 1 bunch fresh basil, chopped
- 1/4 cup small capers
- 2 tablespoons unsalted butter
- 1/2 teaspoon crushed red pepper

1. Cook pasta according to package directions.

2. While the pasta is cooking, heat the oil in a sauté pan. Season the fish on both sides with salt and pepper. Add fish to pan; sauté for 4 to 6 minutes per 1/2-inch thickness of fish, or until the fish flakes when tested with a fork, turning once. Remove fish from pan and set aside.

3. To the same pan add the tomatoes and garlic; cook for 3 minutes more. Add the wine. Bring to boiling. Reduce heat and simmer for 3 minutes.

4. Add the drained cooked pasta, fish, the basil, and capers. Fold in the butter; sprinkle with the crushed red pepper.

NOTE: EXPECT THAT THE FISH WILL BREAK INTO SMALL PIECES TO CREATE THE RUSTIC FEEL OF A FISH RAGOÛT. YOU COULD ALSO TOSS THE PASTA WITH THE BUTTER AND SERVE THE FISH RAGOÛT OVER THE PASTA.

# linguine with lemon cream and sautéed scallops

makes 4 servings

1 pound dried linguine
1 tablespoon olive oil
6 large scallops
Kosher salt and ground black pepper
1 tablespoon minced garlic
1 cup white wine
1 cup heavy cream
Juice of 2 whole lemons (about 1/3 cup)
Pinch saffron threads
Sliced green onion (optional)

1. Cook pasta according to package directions.

2. While the pasta is cooking, heat the oil in a medium sauté pan. Season the scallops with salt and pepper. When the oil is hot add the scallops; sear for 3 minutes on each side until golden brown and opaque. Remove the scallops from pan and set aside.

3. To the same pan add the garlic; sauté for 2 minutes. Add the wine. Bring to boiling. Reduce heat and simmer, uncovered, until liquid is reduced by half. Add the cream, lemon juice, and saffron. Simmer, uncovered, until the liquid is reduced by half and slightly thickened. Season to taste with salt and pepper.

4. Stir in drained cooked pasta; toss to mix well. Top with scallops, garnish with green onion, if desired, and sprinkle with pepper.

# rigatoni with sautéed calamari and fresh tomatoes

makes 4 servings

- 1 pound dried rigatoni pasta
- 9 tubes and tops of small calamari
- 1 tablespoon olive oil
- 1 tablespoon chopped shallot
- 1 tablespoon minced garlic
- 2 vine-ripened tomatoes, finely chopped
- 1 cup white wine
- 1 bunch fresh basil, chopped
- Kosher salt and ground black pepper

1. Cook pasta according to package directions.
2. Cut the tubes of calamari into small rounds.
3. Heat the oil in a medium sauté pan over low heat. Add the calamari, shallot, and garlic; sauté for 2 minutes. Add the tomatoes and wine. Bring to boiling. Reduce heat and simmer until reduced slightly. Add the basil; season to taste with salt and pepper. Serve over cooked rigatoni.

"GREAT FOR A RAINY NIGHT OR A CRAWL-UNDER-A-BLANKET-AND-STAY-IN NIGHT."

# creamed fettuccine with spinach, ricotta, and parmesan cheese

makes 4 servings

- 1 pound dried fettuccine
- 1 tablespoon olive oil
- 1 tablespoon minced garlic
- 1/2 cup white wine
- 1 cup heavy cream
- 2 tablespoons unsalted butter
- 1/4 cup ricotta cheese
- 3 tablespoons finely shredded Parmesan cheese
- Kosher salt and ground black pepper
- 9 ounces fresh spinach

1. Cook pasta according to package directions.

2. While the pasta is cooking, in a medium sauté pan heat the oil over low heat. Add the garlic; sauté for 1 minute. Add the wine. Bring to boiling. Reduce heat and simmer for 2 minutes or until reduced by half. Add the cream and butter; return to boiling. Reduce heat and simmer, uncovered, until slightly thickened. Add the cheeses and season to taste with salt and pepper.

3. Add the drained cooked pasta; toss to combine. Add spinach and toss until spinach is just wilted.

# penne with sweet peas, pancetta, and parmesan

makes 4 servings

- 1 pound dried penne pasta
- 6 slices pancetta
- 1 tablespoon olive oil
- 1 tablespoon minced garlic
- 2 cups heavy cream
- 1½ cups frozen peas
- 2 tablespoons finely shredded Parmesan cheese
- 1 teaspoon chopped fresh thyme
- Kosher salt and ground black pepper

1. Preheat oven to 400°F. Cook the pasta according to package directions.

2. Place pancetta on a baking sheet. Bake 4 to 6 minutes or until crisp. When cool enough to handle, coarsely crumble.

3. Heat the oil in a sauté pan. Add the garlic; sauté over low heat for 1 minute. Add the cream, peas, Parmesan, and thyme. Bring to boiling. Reduce heat and simmer, uncovered, until slightly thickened. Season to taste with salt and pepper.

4. Stir in the drained cooked pasta and pancetta; mix well.

# spaghetti with stewed tomatoes and fresh basil

makes 4 servings

- 1 pound dried spaghetti
- 1 tablespoon olive oil
- 1 cup coarsely chopped plum tomatoes
- 2 tablespoons shaved garlic
- 2 cups white wine
- 1/2 cup red cherry tomatoes, halved
- 1/2 cup yellow cherry tomatoes, halved
- 1 bunch fresh basil, chopped
- 2 tablespoons unsalted butter
- 1/4 cup finely shredded Parmesan cheese
- Kosher salt and ground black pepper

1. Cook the pasta according to package directions.

2. While the pasta is cooking, heat the oil in a medium saucepan over medium heat. Add the plum tomatoes and garlic; cook for 2 minutes. Add the wine, all the cherry tomatoes, and basil. Bring to boiling. Reduce heat and simmer for 5 minutes. Whisk in the butter.

3. Add the drained cooked pasta; mix well. Fold in the cheese and season to taste with salt and pepper.

# 2
# DON'T BE CHICKEN

never underestimate the chicken. There's just so much that you can do with the bird: roast, bake, fry, braise, grill–to mention just a few options. In this chapter I share a few of my favorite, most flavorful chicken dishes that are also surprisingly easy to make. You can use boneless, skinless breasts or bone-in, skin-on breasts–your choice. Just be adventurous with your technique and flavorings. And remember that chicken always makes great leftovers for pastas or sandwiches.

# spicy cashew and scallion chicken

makes 4 to 6 servings

- 1½ pounds skinless, boneless chicken breast halves, cut into 1-inch cubes
- Kosher salt and ground black pepper
- 1 tablespoon cornstarch
- 2 tablespoons olive oil
- 2 tablespoons minced garlic
- ½ teaspoon crushed red pepper
- 2 tablespoons rice vinegar
- 4 tablespoons hoisin sauce
- ¼ cup chicken stock
- 10 scallions (green part) cut into 1-inch pieces
- ¾ cup unsalted cashews (4 ounces)
- Hot cooked white rice (optional)

1. Season chicken with salt and black pepper. In a medium bowl toss chicken with cornstarch until chicken is coated.

2. In a large nonstick skillet heat 1 tablespoon of the oil over medium-high heat. Cook half of the chicken, tossing often, until brown, about 3 minutes. Transfer to a plate. Add remaining 1 tablespoon oil and remaining chicken to skillet along with the garlic and crushed red pepper. Cook, tossing often, until chicken is brown, about 3 minutes.

3. Return first batch of chicken to pan. Add vinegar; cook until evaporated. Add hoisin sauce and chicken stock; cook, tossing, until chicken is cooked through. Remove from heat. Stir in scallions and cashews. Serve immediately over white rice, if desired.

# chicken breasts stuffed with goat cheese, basil, and sun-dried tomatoes

makes 4 servings

- 1/2 cup goat cheese
- 1/2 cup (packed) drained, coarsely chopped oil-packed sun-dried tomatoes
- 1 tablespoon chopped shallot
- 1 teaspoon minced garlic
- 3 or 4 fresh basil leaves, cut in thin strips
- 4 5-ounce boneless chicken breast halves with skin
- Kosher salt and ground black pepper
- 2 tablespoons olive oil
- 1/4 cup butter
- 2 tablespoons lemon juice
- Fresh basil leaves, cut in thin strips

1. Preheat oven to 375°F. In a medium bowl mix goat cheese, tomatoes, shallot, garlic, and the 3 to 4 leaves of basil.

2. Using a small sharp knife and working with one chicken breast at a time, cut a 2-inch-long horizontal slit into the thick side of chicken breast. Move knife back and forth in slit to form a pocket. Divide cheese mixture among chicken pockets. Press edges closed and secure with a toothpick to seal. Sprinkle chicken with salt and pepper.

3. Heat oil in large ovenproof skillet over high heat. Add chicken, skin side down; cook for 2 minutes or until skin is brown. Turn chicken over; transfer skillet to oven. Bake until cooked through (170°F), about 10 minutes.

4. Meanwhile, in a heavy small saucepan melt butter over medium heat. Remove from heat and stir in lemon juice. Slice chicken and place on a serving plate. Drizzle lemon butter over chicken. Garnish with additional basil.

# stir-fry chicken lettuce wraps

makes 4 servings

- 1½ pounds ground chicken breast
- Kosher salt and ground black pepper
- 2 tablespoons olive oil
- 1 large onion, thinly sliced
- 1 large red bell pepper, ribs and seeds removed, thinly sliced
- 1 8-ounce can water chestnuts, rinsed and chopped
- 1½ teaspoons grated fresh ginger
- 3 cloves garlic, minced
- ¼ to ½ teaspoon crushed red pepper
- 3 tablespoons soy sauce
- 3 tablespoons rice vinegar
- 2 tablespoons oyster sauce
- 1½ teaspoons cornstarch, mixed with 1 tablespoon cool water
- 12 to 16 iceberg lettuce leaves, (about 2 heads)

1. Season chicken with salt and black pepper.

2. In a large nonstick skillet, heat 1 tablespoon of the oil over high heat. Add half of the chicken; cook, stirring constantly, until no longer pink, about 2 to 4 minutes. Transfer to a plate. Repeat with remaining chicken. Add remaining tablespoon of the oil to pan, along with the onion, bell pepper, and water chestnuts. Cook, stirring constantly, until onion is golden, about 4 minutes. Reduce heat to medium; add ginger, garlic, and crushed red pepper. Cook, stirring, until fragrant, for 30 to 60 seconds. Stir in soy sauce, vinegar, oyster sauce, and cornstarch mixture; add chicken and any juices. Stir until thickened and bubbly. Serve in lettuce leaves.

# sautéed garlic and parsley chicken

makes 4 servings

- 1 tablespoon olive oil
- 4 airline* chicken breasts, skin on
- 1 teaspoon garlic salt
- 1 teaspoon seasoned salt
- 1/4 teaspoon kosher salt
- 1/2 teaspoon coarsely ground black pepper
- Parsley and Garlic Sauce (see recipe, below)
- Rosemary Potatoes and Carrots (see recipe, page 150)

*NOTE: AN AIRLINE CHICKEN BREAST IS A BONELESS CHICKEN BREAST HALF WITH SKIN AND THE FIRST WING SECTION ATTACHED. A SKIN-ON BONELESS CHICKEN BREAST HALF, OR SKINLESS BONELESS CHICKEN BREAST HALF WILL ALSO WORK FINE FOR THIS RECIPE.

1. Preheat oven to 350°F. In a medium ovenproof sauté pan, heat the oil over medium-high heat. While the oil gets hot, season the chicken with garlic salt, seasoned salt, kosher salt, and pepper. Place the chicken into the oil, skin side down, and sauté for 3 minutes until skin is crispy. Turn the chicken, place in the oven, and cook for another 12 to 15 minutes or until chicken is cooked through (170°F).

2. Serve the chicken hot. Spoon the Parsley and Garlic Sauce over the chicken and serve with Rosemary Potatoes and Carrots.

PARSLEY AND GARLIC SAUCE

In a saucepan bring a small amount of water to boiling; add 1½ bunches fresh flat-leaf parsley. Cook for 2 minutes. Using a slotted spoon quickly remove parsley from water; cool in ice water. Drain on paper towels. In a food processor combine parsley; ½ cup minced garlic; ½ of a bunch fresh rosemary, stems removed; ½ bunch fresh thyme, stems removed; and ½ cup olive oil. Cover and process until smooth. With the food processor running, alternately add 4 ounces fresh baby spinach and 1 cup olive oil, a little at a time, through the feed tube until well combined. Stir in 1 teaspoon kosher salt, 1 teaspoon fresh cracked black pepper, and ½ teaspoon crushed red pepper.

# pan-roasted breast of chicken with morels and arugula

makes 4 servings

- 4 boneless chicken breast halves, skin on
- Kosher salt and ground black pepper
- 1 tablespoon canola oil
- 1 cup diced bacon
- 3/4 pound fresh morel mushrooms
- 2 tablespoons diced shallots
- 2 tablespoons shaved garlic
- 1 cup white wine
- 1 cup chicken stock or broth
- 2 tablespoons unsalted butter
- 4 to 8 arugula leaves

1. Preheat oven to 350°F. Season the chicken on both sides with salt and pepper. In an ovenproof sauté pan heat the oil over medium-high heat. Sear the chicken, skin side down, until skin is nice and crispy. Turn the chicken skin side up and transfer to the oven to cook for 12 to 14 minutes or until chicken is no longer pink. Remove the chicken from pan, cover loosely with foil, and set aside.

2. In the same pan sauté the bacon for 4 minutes or until beginning to crisp. Add the mushrooms, shallots, and garlic; sauté for 2 minutes or until tender. Add the white wine, stirring and scraping to remove any browned bits on the bottom of the pan. Simmer for 2 minutes more. Add the chicken stock; simmer for 4 minutes. Whisk in the butter.

3. Arrange the chicken on a serving platter, spoon the mushroom mixture into the middle of the platter, and place the arugula on top of each piece of chicken.

# pan-fried chicken breast

makes 4 servings

- 1 cup heavy cream
- 4 large egg yolks
- 1 cup fine dry bread crumbs
- 1 cup panko (Japanese-style bread crumbs)
- 1 cup cake flour
- 4 5-ounce skinless, boneless chicken breast halves
- 1 teaspoon garlic salt
- 1 teaspoon seasoned salt
- 1/2 teaspoon ground black pepper
- 1/4 cup canola oil

1. In a medium bowl, stir together the cream and the egg yolks; set aside. In a second bowl combine the two types of bread crumbs. In a third bowl place the flour.

2. Season the chicken with the garlic salt, seasoned salt, and pepper.

3. In a sauté pan heat the oil over low heat. Dip one piece of chicken into the flour, then into the egg mixture, then into the bread crumbs, and finally onto a plate. Repeat with the remaining chicken. Coat all the chicken before you start cooking so that it all cooks evenly.

4. Place the chicken in the heated oil, cook for 4 to 5 minutes on each side so that the chicken turns nice and golden brown, but not too dark. Cook the chicken for 8 to 10 minutes, turning as often as necessary. Lower the heat if the chicken is starting to brown too quickly.

NOTE: FOR THIS PAN-FRIED CHICKEN, BE SURE THAT THE OIL IS HOT BUT NOT SMOKING HOT. YOU WANT TO FRY THE CHICKEN SLOWLY SO THAT IT IS NICE AND FLAKY AND STILL MOIST IN THE CENTER. COOK ONE PIECE FIRST SO YOU CAN GAUGE HOW HOT THE OIL IS AND HOW QUICKLY THE BREAD CRUMBS START TO BROWN.

# pan-roasted garlic and herbed chicken with veggies

makes 6 servings

2 cups olive oil
1 tablespoon chopped fresh tarragon
1 tablespoon chopped fresh sage
1 tablespoon chopped fresh Italian (flat-leaf) parsley
1 tablespoon chopped fresh basil
6 cloves fresh garlic, smashed
2 teaspoons garlic salt
2 teaspoons seasoned salt
6 meaty chicken pieces (assortment of thigh, leg, breast pieces)
Kosher salt and ground black pepper
2 jumbo carrots, peeled and coarsely chopped
2 russet potatoes, peeled and coarsely chopped
2 white onions, coarsely chopped
1 medium celery root (celeriac), peeled and coarsely chopped
2 cups red wine
2 cups chicken stock or broth
6 plum tomatoes, halved

1. For the marinade, in a large bowl combine the oil, herbs, garlic, garlic salt, and seasoned salt. Mix well.

2. Place chicken in a resealable bag set in a shallow bowl. Pour marinade over chicken. Seal bag. Marinate in the refrigerator for 24 hours.

3. Preheat oven to 350°F. Remove chicken from marinade and season with salt and pepper. Discard marinade. Place a large heavy-bottom roasting pan over medium-high heat. Sear chicken on all sides. Stir in carrots, potatoes, onions, and celery root. Stir in wine. Bring to boiling. Reduce heat and simmer 4 minutes or until wine is reduced by half. Stir in chicken broth and return to a boil.

4. Transfer roasting pan to oven; bake for 1 hour. Add tomatoes and bake 15 minutes more or until chicken and vegetables are tender.

# shiitake mushroom chicken with sake and sage

makes 6 servings

6 4-ounce skinless, boneless chicken breast halves
Kosher salt and ground black pepper
1 tablespoon olive oil
2 cups shiitake mushrooms, stems removed and sliced
1 tablespoon chopped fresh sage
6 cloves garlic, thinly sliced
2 cups sake
1 cup chicken stock
3 tablespoons unsalted butter
Fresh sage leaves (optional)

1. Season the chicken with salt and pepper.

2. Heat the oil in a large sauté pan over medium heat. Sauté the chicken for 4 minutes on each side. Add the mushrooms, the chopped sage, and the garlic; sauté for another 3 minutes, or until mushrooms are tender. Add the sake. Bring to boiling. Reduce heat and simmer for 2 minutes. Add the chicken stock; return to a boil. Reduce heat and cook for 4 to 5 minutes more. As the liquid starts to reduce, during the last 2 minutes, stir in the butter and remove from heat.

3. Spoon some of the mushroom mixture and cooking liquid into a shallow dish and top with a chicken breast. Garnish with fresh sage leaves, if desired.

NOTE: THERE ARE MANY TYPES OF SAKE. BE SURE TO GET A GOOD BRAND FOR THIS DISH SO THAT YOU CAN ENJOY THE GREAT FLAVORS THAT A GOOD SAKE CAN BRING. SOME OF MY FAVORITES ARE URAKASUMI ZEN AND GEKKEIKAN HORIN.

# garlic-roasted chicken wings

makes 12 appetizer servings

- 12 organic chicken wings (about 2 pounds)
- 1 tablespoon cooking oil
- 1/4 cup minced garlic
- 1/2 teaspoon seasoned salt
- 1/2 teaspoon poultry seasoning
- Kosher salt and ground black pepper

1. Cut off and discard tips of chicken wings. Cut wings at joints to make 24 pieces.

2. Preheat oven to 375°F. Brush the chicken with oil. Rub the garlic on the chicken pieces and season with seasoned salt, poultry seasoning, salt, and pepper.

3. Line a baking sheet with foil. Place chicken wings on the foil and bake for 35 to 40 minutes or until tender, turning once. Serve with your favorite sauce. such as ranch dressing or barbecue sauce.

# grilled jerk chicken with pineapple salsa

makes 8 servings

- 1 cup vegetable oil
- 1 large yellow onion, chopped
- 1/4 cup red wine vinegar
- 3 green onions, coarsely chopped
- 2 Habañero or Scotch Bonnet chile peppers, stems and seeds removed*
- 2 tablespoons grated fresh ginger
- 2 tablespoons chopped fresh thyme
- 2 tablespoons lime juice
- 1 tablespoon light brown sugar
- 4 cloves garlic, coarsely chopped
- 1 teaspoon ground allspice
- 1/2 teaspoon salt
- 1/4 teaspoon ground black pepper
- 1/4 teaspoon ground cinnamon
- 1/4 teaspoon freshly ground nutmeg
- Pinch ground cloves
- 8 chicken thighs
- 8 drumsticks
- 1 recipe Pineapple Salsa (see recipe, below)

1. For the marinade, in a blender or food processor, combine all the ingredients except the chicken. Cover and blend or puree until almost smooth.

2. Using a fork, make tiny holes in the chicken. Place the chicken in a resealable bag set in a shallow bowl. Pour marinade over chicken. Seal bag. Marinate chicken in the refrigerator for 24 to 48 hours, depending on how intense you want the flavor to be, turning occasionally.

3. Drain chicken, discarding marinade. Place chicken on an uncovered grill directly over medium coals. Grill for 35 to 45 minutes or until cooked through (180°F), turning once. Serve with Pineapple Salsa.

*NOTE: WEAR PLASTIC OR RUBBER GLOVES WHEN HANDLING HOT PEPPERS. THEY HAVE OILS THAT WILL BURN YOUR SKIN AND EYES. IF YOU DO TOUCH THE PEPPERS, WASH YOUR HANDS WITH SOAP AND WATER.

## PINEAPPLE SALSA makes 3 cups

- 2 cups peeled and chopped fresh pineapple
- 1/4 cup finely chopped red onion
- 1/4 cup finely chopped red bell pepper
- 1/4 cup chopped roma tomatoes
- 3 tablespoons lime juice
- 3 tablespoons orange juice
- 2 tablespoons chopped fresh cilantro leaves
- 1 tablespoon chopped green onion
- Salt and freshly ground black pepper to taste

PINEAPPLE SALSA

1. In a medium bowl combine all ingredients. Let stand 30 minutes at room temperature for flavors to blend.

# garlic chicken with roasted tomatoes

makes 3 servings

- 1 cup olive oil
- 2 medium onions, sliced
- 18 cloves garlic, thinly sliced
- 1 tablespoon chopped fresh rosemary
- 1 tablespoon chopped fresh thyme
- 6 chicken thighs
- 2 tablespoons olive oil
- Kosher salt and ground black pepper
- 1 cup red cherry tomatoes
- 1 cup tiny yellow pear tomatoes
- 4 sprigs fresh rosemary
- 4 sprigs fresh thyme

1. For the marinade, in a medium bowl combine the 1 cup oil, half of the onions, half of the garlic, the 1 tablespoon rosemary, and the 1 tablespoon thyme.

2. Place chicken in a resealable bag set in a shallow bowl. Pour marinade over chicken. Seal bag. Marinate the chicken in the refrigerator for 24 hours.

3. Preheat oven to 350°F. In a large heavy roasting pan heat the 2 tablespoons oil. Once the oil is hot, remove the chicken from the marinade, discarding the marinade. Season the chicken with salt and pepper. Place the chicken in the roasting pan, skin side down. Sear the skin for 3 minutes. Turn chicken over and cook for another 4 to 5 minutes, adding the remaining onions and garlic, all the tomatoes, and the rosemary and thyme sprigs. Transfer pan to the oven and roast for 15 to 20 minutes or until chicken is cooked through (180°F).

NOTE: THIS GARLIC CHICKEN IS GREAT SERVED OVER BROWN RICE OR WITH SAUTÉED BROCCOLI.

# roasted ginger, jalapeño and lime chicken

makes 4 servings

- 2 1/2 tablespoons butter, at room temperature
- 1 shallot, finely chopped (about 2 tablespoons)
- 2 tablespoons grated fresh ginger
- 1 tablespoon finely chopped pickled jalapeño chile pepper
- 1 tablespoon lime juice
- 2 teaspoons chili powder
- 1 teaspoon kosher salt
- 1/4 teaspoon ground black pepper
- 1 whole chicken (3 1/2 pounds)
- Kosher salt and ground black pepper
- 2 large onions, thickly sliced
- 1 tablespoon extra-virgin olive oil
- 1 lime, cut into 8 wedges (optional)

1. Preheat oven to 475°F. Make the ginger, jalapeño, lime butter: Using a spoon, in a small bowl mash together 2 tablespoons of the butter, the shallot, ginger, jalapeño, lime juice, chili powder, 1 teaspoon salt, and 1/4 teaspoon black pepper. Set aside.

2. Using your fingers, gently loosen skin from chicken breast. Spoon butter mixture evenly between skin and meat; pat skin back down. Tie chicken legs together with 100 percent cotton kitchen string and tuck wing tips behind the back. Rub chicken with remaining 1/2 tablespoon butter and season with salt and pepper.

3. In a shallow baking pan, arrange onion slices in a single layer; place chicken on top. Roast chicken for 1 1/4 to 1 3/4 hours or until it is nicely brown and an instant-read thermometer inserted in a thigh without touching bone reads 175°F.

4. Transfer chicken to a cutting board and drizzle with olive oil; let stand 10 minutes. In the baking pan, stir onions together with pan juices. Carve chicken; serve with onions and, if desired, lime wedges.

# roasted cornish game hens with citrus marinade

makes 4 servings

- 1/4 cup olive oil
- 4 teaspoons chopped fresh thyme
- 3 garlic cloves, minced
- 2 teaspoons finely shredded fresh lemon peel
- 2 teaspoons finely shredded fresh lime peel
- 1 teaspoon honey
- 1/2 teaspoon salt
- 1/2 teaspoon ground black pepper
- 2 Cornish game hens (1 1/4 to 1 1/2 pounds each), halved lengthwise
- Kosher salt and ground black pepper
- 1 1/2 cups chicken broth
- Lemon and lime wedges (optional)
- Thyme sprigs (optional)

1. For the marinade, in a baking dish stir together olive oil, 3 teaspoons of the thyme, the garlic, lemon peel, lime peel, honey, the 1/2 teaspoon salt, and the 1/2 teaspoon pepper.

2. Using a long heavy knife or kitchen shears, halve the Cornish game hens lengthwise, cutting through the breast bone, just off-center, and through the center of the backbone. Twist wing tips under back. Add hens to marinade; toss to coat. Cover hens and marinate overnight.

3. Preheat oven to 325°F. Transfer hens to another baking dish, discarding marinade. Sprinkle hens with salt and pepper. Add the broth, pouring around the hens, not over them. Cover pan tightly with foil. Roast until hens are cooked through and juices run clear when thighs are pierced with fork, about 1 hour and 15 minutes. Remove from oven. Preheat the broiler.

4. Pour pan juices from hens into a small saucepan; add remaining 1 teaspoon chopped thyme. Bring to boiling. Reduce heat and simmer for 5 minutes or until liquid is reduced to 1 cup (sauce will be thin). Season to taste with salt and pepper.

5. Place hens on an unheated broiler pan. Broil hens 4 to 5 inches from the heat for 4 minutes or until lightly brown, turning once and watching closely to avoid burning. Place 1 hen half on each plate. Spoon sauce over hens and serve. Garnish with lemon and lime wedges and thyme sprigs, if desired.

# 3 BIG BOYS' TOYS

**all right,** *the dishes in this chapter are all about stepping it up—great cuts of meat, special ingredients, and kickin' flavor. Are you game? These main courses are for you, the Harley-riding, stick-smoking, cognac-drinking, off-roading thrill seeker (in reality or in your dreams!) who loves a juicy steak or beautiful roast—but who also wants to take things to the next level. So this weekend, get to the market and pick out some amazing meat. Do it up right on the grill, oven, or range top. Then prepare yourself to eat. I mean really eat!*

# black pepper-crusted colorado rack of lamb

makes 8 to 10 servings

- 4 24-ounce Colorado racks of lamb (6 to 8 ribs each), frenched* and fat removed
- Sea salt
- 2 tablespoons cracked black pepper
- 1/4 cup canola or vegetable oil
- 2 large onions, peeled and roughly chopped
- 20 medium red bee or round red potatoes, roughly chopped
- 1 tablespoon chopped fresh thyme
- 1 tablespoon chopped fresh rosemary

*To french a chop or rack of lamb, part of the meat is removed to expose the end of the bone. If you are uncertain how to do this, ask your butcher to do it for you.

1. Preheat oven to 350°F. Season the racks of lamb well on both sides with sea salt. Sprinkle with black pepper, patting on to adhere. Place a large, heavy roasting pan over medium-high heat; when the pan is hot, add the oil.

2. Sear the lamb loin-side down for 3 to 5 minutes on each side. Turn the racks, bone side down, and transfer to the oven. Roast for 30 minutes.

3. After 30 minutes, add the onions, potatoes, and herbs. Roast 15 minutes more or until an instant read thermometer inserted into the thickest part of the meat reads 128°F (for medium rare) and vegetables are tender. Remove from oven. Cover lamb loosely with foil and let stand for 10 minutes. Slice the lamb into double chops; serve with the onions and potatoes.

**NOTE**: COLORADO LAMB HAS THE REPUTATION OF BEING THE HIGHEST QUALITY LAMB YOU CAN PURCHASE. COLORADO LAMB IS MEATIER, SO WHEN YOU PURCHASE A RACK OF LAMB, A COLORADO RACK OF LAMB WILL BE LARGER THAN A NEW ZEALAND RACK OF LAMB.

# slow-roasted lamb shanks

makes 4 servings

- 4 organic lamb shanks
- 12 cloves garlic, peeled and cut lengthwise in thirds
- Kosher salt
- Seasoned salt
- Ground black pepper
- 4 tablespoons olive oil
- 2 large onions, roughly chopped
- 12 medium red bee or other round red potatoes, quartered
- 1 bunch fresh thyme sprigs
- 1 bunch fresh rosemary sprigs
- 2 cups veal or chicken stock or broth
- 1 teaspoon finely shredded lemon peel (optional)

1. Using a small paring knife, make 3 small slits on 3 sides of each shank; slide a piece of garlic into each slit. Season the lamb with salt, seasoned salt, and pepper. Rub shanks with 2 tablespoons of the oil.

2. Preheat oven to 325°F. Heat the remaining 2 tablespoons oil in a large, heavy roasting pan over medium-high heat. When the oil is very hot but not smoking, sear the lamb on all sides. Add the onions, potatoes, and herbs, stirring to combine.

3. Add the stock, pouring around the meat, not over it. Cover the pan with foil and roast in oven for approximately 2 hours, or until the lamb is fork-tender. Remove the shanks, potatoes, and onions; keep warm.

4. Bring cooking liquid to boiling. Reduce heat and simmer, uncovered, until drizzling consistency. Drizzle shanks with sauce. Sprinkle with lemon peel, if desired.

NOTE: SERVE WITH SAFFRON SUN-DRIED TOMATO RISOTTO OR PARMESAN AND CHEDDAR CHEESE GRITS. (SEE RECIPES, PAGE 16.)

# grilled boneless leg of lamb

makes 8 to 10 servings

- 6 cups olive oil
- 2 white onions, roughly chopped
- 1 cup chopped fresh rosemary
- 1 cup chopped fresh thyme
- 1 cup chopped fresh mint
- 1/4 cup minced garlic
- 1/4 cup diced shallots
- 1/4 cup cracked black pepper
- 1/4 cup honey
- 1/4 cup Dijon mustard
- 1/4 cup lemon juice
- 3 tablespoons brown sugar
- 2 teaspoons kosher salt
- 1 3-pound boneless butterflied lamb leg

1. For the marinade, in a large bowl combine oil, onions, rosemary, thyme, mint, garlic, shallots, pepper, honey, mustard, lemon juice, brown sugar, and salt.

2. Place lamb in a very large resealable bag set in a shallow bowl. Pour marinade over meat. Seal bag. Marinate in the refrigerator for 15 hours, turning lamb occasionally.

3. Drain lamb, discarding marinade. Let lamb stand at room temperature for 30 minutes. The meat should be at room temperature before you start to cook.

4. Place medium-hot coals around a drip pan. Test for medium heat above the pan. Place meat on the grill rack over drip pan. Cover and grill for 50 to 60 minutes or until an instant-read thermometer inserted into the thickest part of the meat reads 135°F for medium-rare.

5. Remove the meat from the grill. Wrap meat in foil; let stand 10 minutes then slice and serve.

NOTE: MARINATING LEG OF LAMB WITH FRESH HERBS AND GARLIC GIVES IT INCREDIBLE FLAVOR. WHEN YOU HAVE COOKED BONELESS LEG OF LAMB ONCE, TRY A BONE-IN LEG OF LAMB FOR AN ENTIRELY DIFFERENT OUTDOOR GRILLING EXPERIENCE.

# lamb and filet stew over cheese grits

makes 4 to 6 servings

- 2 cups cubed beef filet mignon
- 2 cups cubed lamb
- Kosher salt and ground black pepper
- 1/2 cup all-purpose flour
- 1/4 cup olive oil
- 1 red onion, roughly chopped
- 1 cup quartered red bee or other small red potatoes
- 3 jumbo carrots, peeled and rough cut
- 6 cloves garlic, peeled
- 1 1/2 cups canned plum tomatoes
- 1 cup chicken stock or broth
- 2 1/2 cups red wine

1. Preheat oven to 350°F. Season beef and lamb with salt and pepper and/or your favorite seasonings. Dredge the beef and lamb in the flour and shake off the excess. Set aside.

2. Heat the oil in a Dutch oven over medium-high heat. Add the onion, potatoes, carrots, and garlic; sauté for 2 minutes. Add the meat and the tomatoes; sauté for another 2 minutes.

3. Add the stock and the wine. Bring to boiling. Stir, cover, and transfer to oven. Roast slowly for about 1 hour. The meat should be butter-tender; if it is not, return the pot to the oven for another 20 to 30 minutes.

4. Serve over Parmesan and Cheddar Cheese Grits, page 16.

# pan-roasted new york steak with onions and warm spinach

makes 4 servings

- 3 tablespoons cooking oil
- 2 white onions, sliced into ½ inch rounds
- 1 tablespoon minced garlic
- 1 teaspoon chopped fresh rosemary
- 1 teaspoon chopped fresh thyme
- Kosher salt and cracked black pepper
- 4 8-ounce beef New York strip (top loin) steaks
- 2 tablespoons unsalted butter
- 2 tablespoons diced shallots
- 9 ounces fresh spinach

1. Preheat oven to 375°F. Heat 1 tablespoon of the oil in an ovenproof sauté pan over medium heat. Add the onions, garlic, and herbs, and season with salt and pepper. Place the pan in the oven and roast for 15 to 20 minutes or until the onions are golden and tender, turning the onions once.

2. Meanwhile, season the steaks well with salt and pepper. Heat 1 tablespoon of the oil in a sauté pan and cook the steaks over medium heat for 4 minutes on each side or to desired doneness. Remove steaks from pan.

3. In a large sauté pan over medium high heat combine the butter, shallots, and the remaining 1 tablespoon oil. Sauté for 2 minutes or until shallots are just softened. Quickly sauté the spinach, just to wilt it a bit.

4. Slice the steaks; arrange the onions on top of the steak and top with spinach.

# vidalia onion and garlic ribeye steak

makes 4 servings

- 1 24-ounce bone-in beef ribeye steak
- 1/4 cup sea salt
- 1/4 cup freshly cracked black pepper
- 2 tablespoons olive oil
- 8 whole garlic cloves, crushed
- 2 large Vidalia onions, roughly chopped
- 1 bunch fresh rosemary sprigs with stems
- 1 bunch fresh thyme with stems

1. Preheat oven to 350°F. Heavily season the meat on both sides with the salt and pepper, patting them into the meat.

2. Heat the oil in a heavy roasting pan over medium-high heat. Sear the meat for 3 minutes on each side. Remove meat from the pan.

3. Add the garlic, onions, rosemary, and thyme; toss to combine. Return meat to the roasting pan, transfer to the oven, and roast for 18 to 25 minutes for medium rare.

# pan-fried medallions of venison with black truffle mashed potatoes, trumpet mushrooms, and warm bacon reduction

makes 4 servings

- 6 russet potatoes (about 2 pounds), peeled and quartered
- 5 tablespoons unsalted butter
- Kosher salt and ground black pepper
- 1/3 to 1/2 cup milk
- 1 tablespoon black truffle pieces or 1/2 teaspoon truffle oil
- 8 3-ounce venison tenderloin medallions
- 1/4 cup all-purpose flour
- 2 tablespoons olive oil
- 6 slices bacon, finely chopped
- 2 cups black trumpet mushrooms or other wild mushrooms
- 3 tablespoons chopped shallots
- 1 cup white wine
- 1/2 cup chicken stock
- 1 bunch frisée, torn into pieces

*You can find black truffles at gourmet food stores or shop online. Truffle oil is widely available in most supermarket store chains.

1. In a large saucepan cook potatoes, covered, in enough boiling salted water to cover for 20 to 25 minutes or until tender; drain. Mash with a potato masher. Add 3 tablespoons of the butter. Season to taste with salt and pepper. Stir in enough milk to make the mixture light and fluffy. Fold in half of the truffle pieces.

2. Preheat oven to 350°F. Season the venison well on both sides with salt and pepper, then dredge in the flour, shaking off the excess. Heat the oil in an ovenproof sauté pan over medium-high heat. Sauté the meat for 3 minutes on each side. Transfer to the oven for 8 to 12 minutes or to desired doneness.

3. Meanwhile, in a second sauté pan, cook the bacon over low heat for 7 minutes. Add the mushrooms and shallots; sauté for 3 minutes until the mushrooms begin to release their liquid and the bacon gets crisp. Add the wine; simmer for 2 more minutes, then add the stock. Bring to boiling. Reduce heat and simmer, uncovered, for 4 minutes or until slightly thickened. Whisk in the remaining 2 tablespoons butter and the remaining truffle pieces. Keep the sauce warm over low heat.

SERVING SUGGESTION: SPOON FOUR PORTIONS TRUFFLE MASHED POTATOES ON A SERVING PLATTER. PUT ONE VENISON MEDALLION ON EACH PORTION OF POTATOES, THEN DRIZZLE SAUCE OVER ALL. TOP MEAT WITH SOME FRISÉE.

# pan-roasted veal chop with spinach, prosciutto, and sautéed figs

makes 4 servings

- 9 ounces fresh spinach
- 1 tablespoon minced garlic
- 4 tablespoons olive oil
- 4 8-ounce veal rib chops, frenched*
- Kosher salt and ground black pepper
- 1 cup dried or fresh mission figs, halved
- 1/4 cup diced shallots
- 1/4 cup Chambord (raspberry-flavored liqueur)
- 6 tablespoons cold unsalted butter
- 8 slices of prosciutto

1. In a large sauté pan, quickly cook spinach and garlic in 1 tablespoon of the oil until the spinach just wilts; remove from pan and set aside.

2. Preheat oven to 350°F. Season the veal with salt and pepper on both sides. Heat 2 tablespoons of the oil in an ovenproof, very large sauté pan over medium high heat. Sear the chops for 3 minutes per side; transfer to the oven; roast for 10 minutes.

3. Heat the remaining 1 tablespoon oil in another sauté pan placed over medium-high heat. Add the figs and shallots; sauté for 3 minutes until the shallots begin to soften. Carefully add the Chambord; bring to a simmer. Continue cooking until the liquid is reduced by half. Whisk in the butter, 1 tablespoon at a time. Set aside.

4. Remove the chops from the oven and place 2 to 3 tablespoons of wilted spinach on top of each chop. Wrap each chop with two slices of proscuitto. Return chops to sauté pan, return to oven, and cook for another 5 to 7 minutes or to desired doneness. Top each chop with some of the fig mixture and sauce.

*Note: See note on page 67.

# kicked-up bangers and mash

makes 4 servings

- 1 cup diced pancetta
- 1/4 cup olive oil
- 1/2 cup sliced shallots
- 10 pork sausages (bangers), cut into small pieces
- 2 cups trumpet mushrooms
- 1 cup brandy
- 2 tablespoons unsalted butter
- 1 1/2 cups crumbled goat cheese
- 1 recipe Mashed Potatoes (see recipe, below)

1. Heat a medium sauté pan over medium heat. Add pancetta; sauté for 10 to 12 minutes or until pancetta is crispy. Drain off fat. Set aside.

2. Heat the oil in a large sauté pan over medium-high heat. When the oil is hot, add the shallots and sausage; sauté for 3 minutes. Add the mushrooms and brandy; simmer for 1 minute to let the alcohol burn off. Whisk in the butter and remove from heat.

3. Add the crispy pancetta and the goat cheese to the Mashed Potatoes. Serve the mash in a bowl, topped with the bangers and mushroom sauce to finish the dish.

MASHED POTATOES

Wash and peel 5 Idaho potatoes; cut into small cubes. Place potatoes in a pot of cold water with a pinch of salt. Boil for 15 to 20 minutes or until tender. Drain potatoes and return to hot pot. Add 1/2 cup milk, 1/4 cup butter and 1/4 cup heavy cream. Mash potatoes until you have the texture you desire. Season with salt and pepper.

“TO KICK THIS DISH UP, PRESENT IT IN A 4-OUNCE SHOT GLASS. PUT THE PANCETTA IN FIRST, THEN THE MASH, FOLLOWED BY THE SAUSAGE AND MUSHROOMS. FINALLY, TOP WITH A LITTLE GOAT CHEESE.”

# blackened quail with frisée and warm pancetta vinaigrette

makes 4 servings

- 8 quail, butterflied
- 1/4 cup G's Blackening Spice*
- 3 tablespoons olive oil
- 1 cup diced pancetta, cooked crisp
- 2 tablespoons diced shallots
- 1 tablespoon chopped fresh basil
- Kosher salt and ground black pepper
- 8 ounces frisée

1. Preheat oven to 350°F. Season the quail with the blackening spice on all sides.

2. Heat 2 tablespoons of the oil in a large, ovenproof sauté pan over medium-high heat. Sear the quail on all sides, until the skin is light brown in color and slightly crispy, about 5 minutes. Drain, reserving 2 tablespoons of the cooking liquid.

3. Transfer the pan to the oven and roast for 15 to 25 minutes or to desired doneness.

4. Meanwhile, for the vinaigrette, in a medium bowl mix together the pancetta, diced shallots, basil, and the reserved liquid from the quail pan. Whisk in the remaining 1 tablespoon oil, and season with salt and pepper to taste. Place frisée in the middle of a large oval platter, and surround with the quail. Drizzle with the pancetta vinaigrette.

*NOTE: LOOK FOR G'S BLACKENING SPICE AT CHEFGARVIN.COM

# new zealand green mussels with bread crumbs, garlic, and crispy bacon

makes 2 servings

- 1/2 pound New Zealand green mussels or black mussels (about 6 mussels)
- 1 cup salt
- 4 slices bacon, chopped
- 2 tablespoons sliced shallots
- 1 tablespoon shaved garlic
- 1 cup dry white wine
- 2 tablespoons unsalted butter
- 1/2 cup panko (Japanese-style bread crumbs)
- 1/4 cup Italian (flat-leaf) parsley, finely chopped
- Pinch kosher salt

1. Scrub mussels under cold running water. Using your fingers, pull out the beards that are visible between the shells. In an 8-quart Dutch oven combine 4 quarts (16 cups) cold water and 1/3 cup of the salt. Add mussels; soak for 15 minutes. Drain and rinse, discarding water. Repeat twice more.

2. Preheat oven to 400°F. In a hot heavy-bottom roasting pan over medium heat cook bacon, shallots, and garlic until bacon is nearly crisp and shallots and garlic are tender; drain fat. Add the mussels, the white wine, and 1 tablespoon of the butter to the pan; cook until mussels open. Remove mussels from the pan; reserve cooking liquid.

3. In a small microwave-safe bowl heat the remaining 1 tablespoon butter in the microwave on high heat (100 percent power) for 30 to 60 seconds or until melted; stir in the bread crumbs, parsley and the pinch of salt.

4. Remove and discard the top shell of the mussels. Return the mussels to the roasting pan. Spoon a little of the bread crumb mixture on top of each mussel.

5. Place the roasting pan in the oven and bake for 5 minutes or until crumbs are light brown. Keep an eye on the crumbs as they may brown quickly. Remove from the oven. Drizzle reserved cooking liquid over the mussels to serve.

# salt and pepper mussels with jalapeños

makes 2 servings

- 1/2 pound black mussels
- 1 cup salt
- 1 tablespoon cooking oil
- 2 jalapeño chile peppers, sliced into rounds*
- 3 tablespoons chopped fennel bulb
- 2 tablespoons chopped shallots
- 2 tablespoons shaved garlic
- 1 tablespoon unsalted butter
- 1 teaspoon sea salt
- 1 teaspoon cracked white pepper

1. Scrub mussels under cold running water. Using your fingers, pull out the beards that are visible between the shells. In an 8-quart Dutch oven combine 4 quarts (16 cups) cold water and 1/3 cup of the salt. Add mussels; soak for 15 minutes. Drain and rinse, discarding water. Repeat twice more.

2. Preheat oven to 375°F. In an ovenproof sauté pan heat the oil over medium-high heat. Add the mussels; sauté for 1 minute. Add the jalapeños, fennel, shallots, and garlic; sauté for 2 minutes. Add the butter, the 1 teaspoon sea salt, and white pepper.

3. Transfer pan to the oven for 7 minutes or until the mussels open. Serve in the shell.

*NOTE: WEAR PLASTIC OR RUBBER GLOVES WHEN HANDLING HOT PEPPERS. THEY HAVE OILS THAT WILL BURN YOUR SKIN AND EYES. IF YOU DO TOUCH THE PEPPERS, WASH YOUR HANDS WELL WITH SOAP AND WATER.

# steamed black mussels with garlic and cream

makes 2 servings

- 1/2 pound black mussels
- 1 cup salt
- 1 tablespoon cooking oil
- 1/4 cup minced shallots
- 2 tablespoons minced garlic
- 1/4 cup white wine
- 1/2 cup heavy cream
- 1 teaspoon chopped fresh thyme
- 1 tablespoon unsalted butter
- Kosher salt and ground black pepper

1. Scrub mussels under cold running water. Using your fingers, pull out the beards that are visible between the shells. In an 8-quart Dutch oven combine 4 quarts (16 cups) cold water and 1/3 cup of the salt. Add mussels; soak for 15 minutes. Drain and rinse, discarding water. Repeat twice more.

2. In a sauté pan heat the oil over medium-high heat. Add the mussels; sauté for 1 minute. Add the shallots and garlic; sauté for 2 minutes. Add the white wine; cover and simmer for 2 minutes or until mussels open. Add the cream, thyme, and butter. Bring to a simmer. Season to taste with kosher salt and pepper. Serve mussels in the broth.

“THERE'S JUST SOMETHING GREAT ABOUT STEAMING FRESH MUSSELS WITH GARLIC, THE JUICES, AND MAYBE SOME FRENCH FRIES ON THE SIDE–IT'S A BELGIAN THING.”

# sautéed snow crab claws

makes 4 servings

- 1 pound fresh snow crab claws, or frozen snow crab claws, thawed
- Kosher salt and ground black pepper
- 1 tablespoon olive oil
- 1/4 cup white wine
- 1/4 cup small capers
- Juice of 1/2 lemon
- 2 tablespoons unsalted butter
- 1 tablespoon chopped Italian (flat-leaf) parsley (optional)

1. Season the crab claws with salt and pepper on both sides.

2. In a sauté pan, heat oil over medium-high heat. Add the crab; sauté for 3 minutes. Add the wine and simmer for 3 minutes. Add the capers and lemon juice; stir in butter until melted. Sprinkle with parsley, if desired.

# 4
# SEAFOOD, MY FAVORITE

**people ask** all the time what I love to cook. My response is always the same: seafood. So I guess seafood is my favorite. One of the great misconceptions is that cooking fish and seafood is difficult. It is not. To take away your seafood scares, just talk to your fishmonger. Ask when the fish came in, what's the freshest item in the display, and how best to prepare a particular catch. Choose fish with shiny skin, clear eyes, and a fresh smell. Don't cut corners! When you spend the extra time and money for the right fish, you will truly taste your efforts. These recipes are so easy, they almost cook themselves while you watch.

# fresh yellowtail carpaccio with crispy garlic

makes 4 servings

- 2 tablespoons olive oil
- 1/4 cup shaved garlic
- 12 ounces fresh yellowtail or sushi-grade tuna, such as ahi
- 1/2 of a lemon
- Sea salt and cracked white pepper
- 1/4 cup extra-virgin olive oil

1. Heat the 2 tablespoons oil in a sauté pan over medium heat. Add the garlic; sauté for 2 to 3 minutes until crispy and light in color. Remove garlic from the pan and place on a paper towel to drain; set aside.

2. Slice the tuna very thinly and arrange uniformly on an oval platter. Squeeze the lemon half over the fish, then sprinkle with sea salt and white pepper to taste. Top with the crispy garlic and drizzle with the extra-virgin olive oil.

# ahi tuna carpaccio with arugula and black pepper

makes 4 servings

- 1 pound sushi-grade ahi tuna
- 1/4 cup small capers
- 1/2 cup olive oil
- 1/4 cup chopped shallots
- Sea salt and cracked black pepper
- 1 cup arugula

1. Slice the tuna into 1-ounce pieces.

2. On four standard dinner plates place four pieces of tuna spaced evenly apart. Cover each plate completely, even the outer rim, with a large sheet of plastic wrap. Using the flat side of a meat mallet, carefully flatten the tuna on each plate until the tuna completely covers each plate. As you finish each plate, do not remove the plastic; place the tuna in the refrigerator. Once all the tuna is ready, remove the plastic.

3. Place the capers on a cutting board and smash them lightly with the flat side of a chef's knife. In a small bowl combine the capers, oil, and shallots.

4. For each plate, drizzle the caper mixture over the tuna, then sprinkle with sea salt and cracked pepper. Place arugula in the center of the plate.

“THERE'S NOTHING LIKE THE TASTE OF FRESH TUNA WITH CRACKED PEPPER, A LITTLE OLIVE OIL, CAPERS, AND SOME FRESH LEMON.”

# mahi mahi
## with lobster ragoût

makes 4 servings

- 4 6-ounce skinless mahi mahi fillets
- Kosher salt and ground black pepper
- Olive oil
- 1 2-pound lobster, cooked, shelled, and diced
- 2 tablespoons diced shallots
- 1 cup trumpet mushrooms, coarsely chopped
- 1 cup white wine
- 2 tablespoons unsalted butter
- 2 tablespoons chopped parsley
- 1/4 cup bread crumbs

1. Preheat oven to 325°F. Season the fish with salt and pepper on both sides. Heat the oil in a sauté pan over medium-high heat. Add the mahi-mahi; sauté for 3 to 4 minutes on one side. Remove fish from the pan; set aside.

2. Add the lobster, the shallots, and mushrooms to the same pan; sauté for 3 minutes. Add the wine; bring to a simmer. Fold in the butter and parsley.

3. Place the fish in a greased baking pan and top each fillet with 2 tablespoons of the lobster ragoût. Sprinkle each fillet with bread crumbs; bake the fish for 3 to 5 minutes or until fish begins to flake when tested with a fork.

# poached red snapper with avocado, white peach, and cilantro salsa

makes 4 servings

- 3 to 4 cups water
- 1 cup white wine
- juice of 2 lemons
- Kosher salt
- 4 4-ounce red snapper fillets, skin on
- 1/4 cup peeled, diced white peaches or regular peaches
- 1/4 cup diced avocado
- 2 tablespoons diced shallots
- 1 bunch fresh cilantro, coarsely chopped

1. Combine the water, wine, and half of the lemon juice in a medium-size sauté pan; add a pinch or two of salt, to taste. Bring to a simmer and check the seasoning. Add the fish and cook gently for 5 to 7 minutes.

2. Meanwhile, in a medium bowl, mix together the peaches, avocado, shallots, and cilantro. Stir in the remaining lemon juice. Remove fish from the poaching broth and top each fillet with spoonful of the peach salsa.

“ ;EACH, PARK, OR POOLSIDE PICNIC
VITH THIS DISH–IT'S A BANGER. ”

# pan-seared snapper with goat cheese gnocchi and saffron broth

makes 4 servings

- 4 8-ounce boneless Japanese or red snapper fillets, skin on, cut in half on a bias
- Kosher salt and ground black pepper
- 1/4 cup olive oil
- 2 cups white wine
- 1/2 cup heavy cream
- 1 teaspoon saffron threads
- 3 tablespoons unsalted butter
- 4 ounces plain potato gnocchi
- 1 ounce goat cheese

1. Preheat oven to 325°F. Season the snapper fillets on both sides with salt and pepper, and score the skin.

2. Heat olive oil in an ovenproof sauté pan over medium-high heat. Place the fish, skin side down, in the pan and sear until crispy. Transfer the pan to the oven and continue to cook for another 5 minutes. While the fish is cooking, bring a large pot of salted water to boiling.

3. Remove pan from the oven, place fish on a platter, and loosely cover with foil to keep warm. Set the pan over medium-high heat, pour in the white wine, and bring to a simmer. Simmer, uncovered, for 2 minutes. Add the cream and saffron; continue to cook, reducing the sauce until it is thick enough to cling to the back of a spoon. Whisk in 2 tablespoons of the butter and season to taste. Strain the sauce through a fine mesh sieve into a bowl. Return the strained sauce to pan.

4. Add the gnocchi to the boiling water; boil until they float to the surface of the water. Drain and return to the pan with the remaining tablespoon of butter. Blend in the goat cheese, and adjust the seasoning, if necessary. Serve gnocchi with the fish and sauce.

SERVING SUGGESTION: SERVE THE SNAPPER TO ONE SIDE OF THE PLATE. PLACE THE GNOCCHI IN A SMALL RICE BOWL, AND PRESENT THE SAFFRON SAUCE IN A SHOT GLASS OR SMALL DISH NEXT TO THAT. IF YOU LIKE, DRIZZLE WITH BALSAMIC REDUCTION AND GREEN OIL FOR STYLE AND COLOR. (SEE RECIPES, PAGE 15)

# pan-seared chilean sea bass with crispy onions and chive beurre blanc

makes 4 servings

- 4 4-ounce Chilean sea bass fillets, skin on
- Kosher salt and ground black pepper
- 1 tablespoon olive oil
- 3 tablespoons chopped chives
- Beurre Blanc (see recipe, below)
- 1 recipe Crispy Onions (see recipe, below)

1. Season the fish on both sides with salt and pepper. Heat oil in a sauté pan over medium-high heat. Place the fish, skin-side down, in the pan and cook until the skin is crispy. Turn the fish, reduce the heat to medium and continue to cook for 4 to 6 minutes total per ½-inch thickness of fish, or until fish flakes when tested with a fork.

2. Stir chives into Beurre Blanc. Spoon some Beurre Blanc onto each serving plate. Place fish over sauce. Top with Crispy Onions.

### BEURRE BLANC

In a medium saucepan combine ½ cup white wine, ¼ cup diced shallots, and 2 tablespoons white wine vinegar. Bring to boiling. Reduce heat and boil gently for 8 to 10 minutes or until reduced to ¼ cup. Cut 3 sticks of cold butter into 2-tablespoon pieces. Set aside. Whisk in 3 tablespoons heavy cream, then the butter, 1 piece at a time. Add the next piece only after the butter melts each time. Strain sauce, if desired, through a fine mesh sieve. Season to taste with salt and pepper.

### CRISPY ONIONS

Thinly slice 1 onion. Season with ½ teaspoon salt and black pepper. Place ½ cup cornstarch in a bowl. Add onions and toss to coat well with cornstarch. In a frying pan, heat 1 inch of canola oil to 365°F. Fry a few onions in the oil at a time until golden brown. Use a slotted spoon to remove onions from oil. Place on paper towels to absorb excess oil.

# eggs benedict with blackened sea bass and prosciutto

makes 8 servings

- 1 tablespoon olive oil
- 1 pound sea bass, cut into 8 portions
- 1 tablespoon G's Blackening Spice*
- cup white vinegar
- Pinch kosher salt
- 8 eggs
- 1 tablespoon butter, softened
- 4 English muffins, split
- 8 slices prosciutto
- 1 cup Hollandaise Sauce (see recipe, below)
- Fresh Italian (flat-leaf) parsley leaves

1. Preheat oven to 350°F. Heat the oil in a sauté pan over medium heat. Lightly season fish with the blackening spice on both sides; sauté for 4 to 6 minutes per ½-inch thickness of fish or until the fish flakes when tested with a fork, turning once.

2. While the fish is cooking, bring a large pot of water to boiling, add the vinegar and a pinch of salt. Reduce heat to a simmer. Break one of the eggs into a measuring cup. Hold the cup as close to the water as you can and carefully slide the egg into the water. Repeat with the remaining eggs. Simmer 4 to 6 minutes for a medium poach (the whites should be set and the yolks thickened).

3. Meanwhile, spread the butter on insides of the muffins. Place muffins on a baking sheet and bake about 5 minutes or until toasted.

4. Place one portion of fish on each muffin half. Put one slice of prosciutto on top of the fish, one poached egg on top of the prosciutto, and one tablespoon of Hollandaise Sauce on each egg. Garnish with parsley.

HOLLANDAISE SAUCE

Cut ½ cup unsalted butter into thirds and bring it to room temperature. In the top of a double boiler, combine 3 beaten egg yolks, 1 tablespoon lemon juice, and 1 tablespoon water. Add a piece of butter, place over, but not touching, gently boiling water. Cook whisking quickly until butter melts. Add the remaining butter, a piece at a time, stirring constantly until butter melts each time. Cook for 2 minutes or until sauce thickens. Season to taste with salt and pepper.

"
.OOK FOR MY BLACKENING
PICE ON CHEFGARVIN.COM
"

# blackened flat-grilled chilean sea bass skewers

makes 4 servings

- 8 to 10 (4-inch) wooden skewers
- 1 pound fresh Chilean sea bass, cod, or whitefish (cut into small cubes)
- 1/4 cup G's Blackening Spice*
- 2 tablespoons olive oil
- Lemon wedges (optional)

1. Soak skewers in water for at least 30 minutes.
2. Place 3 to 4 pieces of sea bass on each skewer, leaving no space between the fish pieces.
3. Place the blackening spice in a shallow dish. Dredge the fish skewers in the seasoning to coat fish cubes on all sides.
4. Heat the oil in a grill pan over medium-high heat. Place the fish on the grill pan and sear on all sides, turning repeatedly until fish flakes when tested with a fork, about 8 to 12 minutes. Serve with lemon wedges, if you like.

NOTE: G'S BLACKENING SPICE IS AVAILABLE AT CHEFGARVIN.COM

# poached atlantic salmon with fresh cucumber and mint salad

makes 6 servings

- 2 cups white wine
- 1 cup sake
- 1 cup water
- 1/4 cup rice vinegar
- 6 4-ounce skinless salmon portions
- Kosher salt and ground white pepper
- 3 English cucumbers, peeled and julienned
- 1 bunch fresh mint, coarsely chopped
- 1/2 cup olive oil

1. In a Dutch oven combine the wine, sake, water, and 2 tablespoons of the vinegar. Bring to boiling.

2. Season the fish on both sides with salt and white pepper; place in the poaching liquid. Reduce heat. Simmer fish, covered, for 4 to 6 minutes per 1/2-inch thickness of fish, or until fish flakes when tested with a fork.

3. For the salad, mix the cucumbers and mint in bowl. Add the remaining vinegar, the oil, and a pinch of salt and white pepper. Mix well.

4. Serve the cucumber salad with a slotted spoon. Place the salmon on top of the salad.

# pan-seared crispy salmon with buttered leeks and fava beans

makes 4 servings

- 4 6-ounce salmon fillets, with skin
- Kosher salt and ground black pepper
- 3 tablespoons olive oil
- 1 teaspoon minced garlic
- 2 tablespoons diced shallot
- 1 large leek, white part only, washed well and diced
- 1½ cups shelled fresh fava beans, cooked
- 2 cups white wine
- 1 tablespoon unsalted butter

1. Season the fish on both sides with salt and pepper. Heat 2 tablespoons of the olive oil in a sauté pan. Place the salmon, skin-side down, in the pan and cook (without moving the fish) until the skin is crispy, about 4 to 5 minutes. Reduce the heat, turn the salmon, and continue to cook for another 3 to 4 minutes.

2. Meanwhile, heat the remaining 1 tablespoon oil in another sauté pan over medium heat. Add the garlic, shallots, and leek; sauté for 3 to 5 minutes until the leek begins to soften.

3. Add the fava beans and the wine; bring to a gentle simmer. Add the butter. Season to taste with salt and pepper.

SERVING SUGGESTION: PLACE THE LEEK AND BEAN MIXTURE ON EACH PLATE AND TOP WITH THE SALMON (SKIN SIDE UP). DRIZZLE WITH A DROP OF OLIVE OIL.

# warm fish tacos

makes 4 to 6 servings

- 8 to 12 ounces tilapia or Dover sole
- Kosher salt and ground black pepper
- 2 tablespoons olive oil
- 2 tablespoons unsalted butter
- 1 package 6-inch flour tortillas
- Prepared guacamole
- Diced tomato
- Diced red onion
- Chopped fresh cilantro

1. Season the fish on both sides with salt and pepper. Heat oil and 1 tablespoon of the butter together in a sauté pan over medium-high heat. Sauté the fish 2 minutes on each side, until it has a crispy brown crust. Remove from the heat.

2. In a separate sauté pan set over medium-low heat, melt the remaining tablespoon of butter. Lightly toast the tortillas on both sides. Keep them warm on a plate by covering with a clean kitchen towel.

3. Using a fork, flake the fish and place a small amount on each tortilla. Top with guacamole, tomatoes, onions, and cilantro; roll up.

SERVING SUGGESTIONS: FEEL FREE TO USE AS MUCH OR AS LITTLE TOMATO, GUACAMOLE, ONIONS, AND CILANTRO AS YOU WOULD LIKE.

# trio niçoise salad

makes 4 servings

- 2 medium red bee or other small red potatoes
- 4 ounces haricots verts (French green beans)
- 4 ounces salmon
- 4 ounces halibut
- 4 ounces ahi tuna
- Kosher salt and ground black pepper
- 4 tablespoons olive oil
- 1 tablespoon Dijon mustard
- Juice of 1 lemon
- 2 shallots, diced
- 8 to 10 ounces mixed greens
- 3 red cherry tomatoes
- 3 yellow cherry tomatoes
- 2 whole eggs, hard-boiled, peeled, and quartered
- 1/2 cup niçoise olives, pitted

1. Bring a small saucepan of water to boiling. Add the potatoes; cook for 10 to 12 minutes until the potatoes are soft. Drain, and plunge potatoes into a bowl filled with ice water to cool. Drain again and set aside.

2. In a medium saucepan bring salted water to boiling. Add the green beans and cook for 5 to 8 minutes. Drain, and plunge beans into a bowl filled with ice water to cool. Drain again and set aside.

3. Season all the fish with salt and pepper. Heat 2 tablespoons of the olive oil in a sauté pan over medium-high heat. Starting with the salmon and the halibut, sauté the fish for 2 minutes on each side. Add the tuna; sauté for 2 minutes on each side while the salmon and halibut remain in the pan. Remove from the heat. When cool enough to handle, flake the fish.

4. For the vinaigrette, in a medium bowl mix together the Dijon mustard, the lemon juice , a pinch of salt, and the shallots. Slowly add the remaining 2 tablespoons oil and whisk well.

5. Place the mixed greens in the center of a medium oval platter. Slice the potatoes and the tomatoes and place around the greens, along with the green beans, the eggs, and the olives. Top with the fish, and drizzle with the vinaigrette.

# baked alaskan halibut with fresh herbs and roasted red bee potatoes

makes 6 servings

- 1/2 pound red bee or other small round red potatoes, quartered
- 1/4 cup olive oil
- 6 4-ounce portions halibut
- Kosher salt and ground black pepper
- 3 tablespoons diced shallots
- 3 tablespoons minced garlic
- 1 tablespoon chopped fresh rosemary
- 1 tablespoon chopped fresh thyme
- 1 tablespoon chopped fresh mint

1. Preheat oven to 350°F. In a large saucepan, cook potatoes in boiling salted water for 5 minutes; drain.

2. Spread 3 tablespoons of the oil over a baking pan. Season the fish with salt and pepper; place fish on the oiled baking pan.

3. In a small bowl mix together 2 tablespoons of the shallots, 2 tablespoons of the garlic, the rosemary, thyme, and mint. Coat each piece of fish generously with the herb mixture. Bake the fish in the oven for 4 to 6 minutes per 1/2-inch thickness of fish, or until the fish flakes easily when tested with a fork.

4. For the potatoes, in a sauté pan heat the remaining 1 tablespoon oil over medium heat. Add the remaining 1 tablespoon shallots, the remaining 1 tablespoon garlic, and if there are herbs left, add them as well; cook about 1 minute or until fragrant. Add the potatoes and sauté for 7 minutes or until nice and crisp outside and tender inside. Serve potatoes with the fish.

# grilled swordfish with sun-dried tomatoes, kalamata olives, and capers

makes 4 servings

- 4 6-ounce swordfish steaks
- Kosher salt and ground black pepper
- 1/4 cup olive oil
- 1 tablespoon diced shallot
- 10 ounces sun-dried tomatoes (not oil-packed)*
- 3/4 cup kalamata olives, pitted
- 1/2 cup capers, drained and rinsed in water
- 1/2 cup bread crumbs

*SOAK DRIED SUN-DRIED TOMATOES IN WARM WATER FOR 10 MINUTES PRIOR TO USING THEM.

1. Preheat a grill or, if you are uisng a grill pan, place it over medium-high heat. Season the swordfish on both sides with salt and pepper.

2. Preheat oven to 325°F. Heat the oil in a sauté pan over medium-high heat; add shallot, tomatoes, olives, and capers. Cook for 3 to 5 minutes, until the olives and capers have softened.

3. Meanwhile place the fish on the grill; cook for 4 minutes. Turn the fish and cook for 4 minutes more. Remove the fish to an ovenproof plate or platter, top with the tomato mixture and the bread crumbs, and place in the oven for 3 minutes.

SERVING SUGGESTION: THIS VERY QUICK AND EASY SWORDFISH DISH GOES GREAT WITH ASPARAGUS TIPS. OR YOU COULD DO A VERY SIMPLE TWO-CHEESE RISOTTO TO KICK IT UP.

# grilled swordfish with sautéed bay shrimp and crab

makes 4 servings

- 4 6-ounce swordfish steaks
- Kosher salt and ground black pepper
- 2 tablespoons olive oil
- 2 tablespoons diced shallots
- 2 tablespoons diced garlic
- 1/4 cup fresh bay shrimp
- 1/4 cup lump crabmeat
- 3 tablespoons capers, rinsed and drained

1. Preheat a grill or, if you are using a grill pan, place it over medium-high heat. Season the swordfish on both sides with salt and pepper.

2. Grill the fish over medium heat, and move it frequently to keep it from burning, about 3 to 5 minutes on one side. Turn the fish and grill for another 3 to 5 minutes.

3. Meanwhile heat the oil in a sauté pan over medium-high heat. Add the shallots, garlic, shrimp, crab, and capers. Sauté for 3 to 4 minutes and taste for seasoning. Top each swordfish steak with the crab and shrimp mixture.

# grilled shrimp breakfast cocktail

makes 4 servings

- 2 cups Parmesan and Cheddar Cheese Grits (see recipe, page 16)
- Oil for deep-fat frying
- 4 wonton wrappers
- 8 medium shrimp, peeled and deveined
- Kosher salt and ground black pepper
- Seasoned salt
- 6 organic eggs, lightly beaten
- 1/4 cup heavy cream
- 2 tablespoons chopped green onion
- 2 tablespoons butter
- 4 slices pancetta, cooked crisp
- Green onions, cut in thin strips

1. Prepare Parmesan and Cheddar Cheese Grits; keep warm.

2. Add 1 inch of oil to a small saucepan. Heat the oil over medium heat to 365°F or until a bread cube dropped in the oil browns quickly. Add one wonton wrapper to the saucepan. Cook until browned and crisp. Drain on paper towels. Repeat with remaining wonton wrappers.

3. Season shrimp with salt, pepper, and seasoned salt. Grill shrimp over medium heat for 5 to 8 minutes or until opaque, turning once. Remove from grill and keep warm.

4. Break the eggs into a medium bowl. Add the cream; mix well. Stir in 2 tablespoons chopped green onion. In a medium sauté pan melt butter over medium heat. Add egg mixture; cook without stirring until eggs begin to set. With a spatula, lift and fold the partly cooked mixture so the uncooked part moves to the bottom of the pan. Continue cooking and folding until mixture is cooked through but still looks moist. Season with salt and pepper and remove from the heat.

5. On a serving plate place a wonton crisp. Top with 1/2 cup grits, a slice of pancetta, some of the scrambled egg, and a grilled shrimp. Garnish with green onion. Repeat for remaining servings.

NOTE: THIS IS A VERY EASY RECIPE. BE SURE TO COOK THE PANCETTA, THE WONTONS, AND THE GRITS AHEAD OF TIME SO THAT THIS DISH IS SERVED HOT.

# seafood ragoût with saffron broth and haricots verts

makes 4 servings

- 4 New Zealand green mussels or black mussels
- 4 clams
- 1 cup salt
- 3 tablespoons olive oil
- 3 tablespoons chopped shallots
- 1/3 cup chopped fresh fennel
- Pinch saffron
- 1 1/2 cups white wine
- 1 tablespoon unsalted butter
- 1/2 cup Beurre Blanc (see recipe, page 96)
- 8 ounces sea bass, cut into four 2-ounce portions
- 4 large sea scallops
- 4 jumbo shrimp, peeled and deveined
- Kosher salt and ground black pepper
- 1 1/2 cups haricots verts (French green beans)

1. Scrub mussels and clams under cold running water. Using your fingers, pull out the beards that are visible between the mussel shells. In an 8-quart Dutch oven combine 4 quarts (16 cups) cold water and 1/3 cup salt. Add mussels and clams; soak for 15 minutes. Drain and rinse, discarding water. Repeat twice more.

2. In a Dutch oven heat 1 tablespoon of the oil over medium-high heat. Add mussels and clams; sauté for 1 minute. Add 2 tablespoons of the shallots; continue cooking until shellfish opens. Remove shellfish from pan; set aside.

3. Put pan back over the heat. Add the fennel and saffron; sauté for 3 minutes or until tender. Add wine; bring to boiling. Reduce heat and simmer for 2 minutes. Whisk in the butter. Add the Beurre Blanc; simmer 3 more minutes or until desired consistency.

4. While the sauce is simmering, season the sea bass, scallops, and shrimp with salt and pepper. Heat 1 tablespoon of the oil in a sauté pan over high heat. Add the bass, scallops, and shrimp. Sauté until scallops and shrimp are opaque and bass flakes when tested with a fork, 4 to 6 minutes.

5. Put the mussels, clams, bass, scallops, and shrimp in the Dutch oven with the sauce; simmer to heat through. Serve on a large platter.

6. In a sauté pan heat remaining 1 tablespoon oil. Add the haricots verts and the remaining shallots to the pan; sauté over medium-high heat until beans are just tender. Place bean mixture in the middle of the seafood ragoût.

# cast iron-roasted seafood sizzle with lemon

makes 4 servings

1 small lobster tail, removed from its shell
2 ounces Chilean sea bass
2 ounces salmon
4 large sea scallops
4 large prawns or jumbo shrimp, peeled, deveined, and split lengthwise
4 New Zealand mussels, scrubbed
4 ounces cleaned calamari
4 Manila clams
Kosher salt and ground black pepper
4 tablespoons olive oil
1 large Meyer lemon, cut in half

1. Preheat oven to 375°F. Season all the seafood with salt and pepper. Heat a very large, dry cast-iron skillet over medium-high heat. Heat 2 tablespoons of the olive oil.

2. Sear the lobster, sea bass, salmon, scallops, and prawns for 2 minutes on one side; turn. Add the mussels, calamari, and clams. Squeeze half the lemon over the seafood and place in the oven for 5 minutes.

3. Remove from the oven, and squeeze the remaining half lemon over the seafood. Drizzle with the remaining 2 tablespoons oil.

SERVING SUGGESTION: THIS DISH CAN BE SERVED DIRECTLY FROM THE SKILLET, ACCOMPANIED BY A BOWL OF RICE OR A SIMPLE SALAD. BE SURE TO SET THE CAST-IRON SKILLET ON A TRIVET, TABLE COASTER, OR HEATPROOF PLACE MAT.

# seafood pot pie

makes 6 servings

- 2 tablespoons olive oil
- 2 tablespoons diced shallot
- 6 ounces crab meat
- 6 ounces lobster meat
- 6 ounces Chilean sea bass, cut into 1-ounce portions
- 6 ounces salmon, cut into 1-ounce portions
- 6 ounces halibut, cut into 1-ounce portions
- 8 jumbo shrimp, peeled and deveined, each cut into 4 small pieces
- 6 jumbo sea scallops, cut into quarters
- Kosher salt and ground black pepper
- 1 teaspoon vanilla extract
- 2 cups asparagus tips
- 1 cup peeled and diced red bee or other small round red potatoes
- 1 cup fresh sweet corn kernels
- 1 cup sweet peas
- 1/2 cup diced celery
- 1 cup peeled and diced red bee or other small round red potatoes
- 4 cups lobster stock
- 2 cups heavy cream
- 1/2 of a 17.3-ounce package frozen puff pastry sheets
- 1 egg, beaten and whisked with 2 tablespoons water

1. Heat the oil in a large pot over medium-high heat; add the shallots. Season all the seafood with salt and pepper and add to the pot. Sear the seafood for 2 minutes.

2. Preheat oven to 350°F. Add the vanilla, all the vegetables and potatoes to the pot, followed by the lobster stock and the cream. Bring to a simmer. Simmer for 5 minutes.

3. Ladle the stew into six individual 4-ounce baking dishes. Cover with the puff pastry, cutting away excess pastry with kitchen scissors. Brush the pastry with the egg wash mixture. Place pies on a cookie sheet in the oven. Bake for 10 to 12 minutes or until pastry is golden.

# scallop ceviche
## with avocado

makes 6 servings

- 8 to 10 large sea scallops
- 4 medium roma tomatoes, finely chopped
- 1 medium red onion, finely chopped
- 1 medium hot chile pepper, (such as Anaheim or poblano), seeded and chopped*
- 1/3 cup lemon juice
- 3 tablespoons olive oil
- 2 tablespoons chopped fresh cilantro
- Kosher salt and ground white pepper
- 1/2 cup finely chopped avocado

1. Chop the scallops into small pieces and place in a large bowl. Add the tomatoes, onion, hot pepper, lemon juice, olive oil, and cilantro. Season the mixture to taste with salt and pepper.

2. Place about 1 tablespoon of avocado into 6 martini glasses. Spoon the ceviche on top of the avocado.

*Note: See note on page 59.

NOTE: START WITH "SUPER FRESH" SCALLOPS FOR THIS KICKIN' DISH. LOOK FOR SCALLOPS THAT HAVE A SWEET SMELL AND A FRESH MOIST SHEEN. REFRIGERATE IMMEDIATELY AFTER YOU BUY THEM AND USE THEM WITHIN A DAY OR TWO.

# lump crab and shrimp
## with avocado and greens

makes 6 servings

- 8 ounces lump crabmeat
- 1 cup cooked, peeled, and diced shrimp
- 1/4 cup diced celery
- 1/4 cup diced hard-boiled egg whites
- 2 tablespoons mayonnaise
- 1/2 small lemon, juiced
- Kosher salt and ground black pepper
- 1 avocado, peeled, pitted, and diced
- 2 teaspoons olive oil
- 4 ounces micro or baby greens
- Crackers

1. In a large bowl, mix together the crabmeat, shrimp, celery, and egg whites. Add the mayonnaise and blend well to incorporate. Squeeze in the lemon juice and season to taste with salt and pepper.

2. Season the avocado with salt and pepper; toss with 1 teaspoon of the olive oil. Toss the greens with the remaining 1 teaspoon of olive oil. See serving suggestion below.

SERVING SUGGESTION: USING A MEDIUM-SIZE RING MOLD, PLACE THE AVOCADO ON THE BOTTOM, THEN THE CRAB SALAD, AND PRESS UNTIL FIRM. REMOVE THE MOLD AND TOP WITH THE GREENS. DRIZZLE WITH ADDITIONAL OIL. SERVE WITH CRACKERS.

# calamari-rock shrimp salad with frisée

makes 4 servings

- 12 ounces fresh calamari, cleaned and cut into small pieces or frozen calamari, thawed*
- Kosher salt and ground black pepper
- 2 tablespoons olive oil
- 1 teaspoon minced garlic
- 1 teaspoon diced shallots
- 6 ounces rock shrimp
- 1/2 cup red teardrop tomatoes
- 1/2 cup yellow teardrop tomatoes
- 2 cups white wine
- 2 tablespoons unsalted butter
- 1 tablespoon heavy cream
- 2 tablespoons chopped green onions
- 2 bunches frisée

1. Season the calamari with salt and pepper. Place a sauté pan over medium-high heat, and when the pan is hot, add the oil. Add the garlic and shallots; cook for 1 minute.

2. Add the shrimp and tomatoes to the pan; sauté for 2 minutes. Add the wine, stir, and simmer for 2 minutes. Add the butter and cream, stirring to incorporate. Continue to simmer for 2 minutes more. Add the green onions and remove from heat.

3. Use a slotted spoon to transfer the calamari, shrimp, and tomatoes to a large bowl or deep platter. Continue to simmer the cooking liquid for 1 to 2 more minutes. Place the frisée on top of the seafood; drizzle some of the sauce around the salad.

*NOTE: IF YOU PURCHASE FRESH CALAMARI, THE FISHMONGER WILL CLEAN IT FOR YOU. IF YOU'RE INTENT TO CLEAN IT YOURSELF, PULL HEADS AND TENTACLES OUT OF CALAMARI BODIES. CUT HEADS OFF TENTACLES AND DISCARD HEADS. REMOVE AND DISCARD ANY ENTRAILS THAT REMAIN IN THE BODIES. PULL OUT AND DISCARD THE CLEAR CARTILAGE "PEN" RUNNING DOWN THE BACK OF THE BODIES. WITH YOUR FINGERS, PEEL SKIN OFF OUTSIDE OF BODIES. RINSE BODIES AND TENTACLES; PAT DRY. CUT BODIES INTO RINGS. FROZEN CALAMARI IS ALREADY CLEANED.

# sautéed calamari with cherry tomatoes, black mussels and clams

makes 4 servings

- 8 black mussels
- 8 small clams
- 1 cup salt
- 2 cups calamari, cleaned and cut into small pieces*
- 1 tablespoon cooking oil
- 1 tablespoon chopped shallot
- 1 tablespoon shaved garlic
- 2 cups white wine
- 6 red cherry tomatoes, halved
- 6 yellow cherry tomatoes, halved
- Pinch saffron
- 2 tablespoons unsalted butter
- Kosher salt and ground black pepper

1. Scrub mussels and clams under cold running water. Using your fingers, pull out the beards that are visible between the shells of the mussels. In an 8-quart Dutch oven combine 4 quarts (16 cups) cold water and 1/3 of the salt. Add mussels and clams; soak for 15 minutes. Drain and rinse, discarding water. Repeat twice more.

2. In a large sauté pan heat oil over medium-high heat. Add the shallot, garlic, mussels, and clams; sauté for 2 minutes. Add the calamari, wine, cherry tomatoes, and the saffron. Bring to boiling. Reduce heat and simmer, covered, for 5 minutes, or until clams and mussels open. Stir in the butter; season with salt and pepper.

3. To serve, arrange the mussels as the outer row on a platter, then the clams and the calamari in the middle. Pour the saffron broth over the shellfish. *Note: See cleaning note on opposite page.

# sautéed skate wing over crab cakes with wasabi mayo

makes 6 servings

- Maryland Crab Cakes (see recipe, page 119)
- 6 4-ounce portions skate wing
- Kosher salt and ground white pepper
- 1/4 cup all-purpose flour
- 1 tablespoon canola oil
- 2 egg yolks
- 2 tablespoons lemon juice
- 2 teaspoons white vinegar
- 1 cup canola oil
- 1 1/2 tablespoons wasabi paste
- 1 cup arugula

1. Prepare and cook the Maryland Crab Cakes; keep warm.

2. Season the fish with salt and pepper. Place the flour in a shallow dish. Dredge the fish in the flour, patting off the excess. Heat the 1 tablespoon oil in a sauté pan. Add the fish; sauté for 4 to 6 minutes per 1/2-inch thickness of fish or until fish flakes when tested with a fork, turning once.

3. For the wasabi mayo, in a medium bowl combine the egg yolks, 1 tablespoon of the lemon juice, the vinegar, and a pinch of salt and pepper. Whisk together. Slowly pour in the 1 cup oil in a thin steady stream, whisking constantly to emulsify. Add wasabi paste and remaining lemon juice to taste.

4. Place two Crab Cakes on each dinner plate, put one piece of fish on top of the crab cakes, top with the mayo, then put a few arugula leaves on top.

# maryland crab cakes

makes 12 crab cakes

- 1 pound lump crabmeat
- 3 tablespoons Dijon mustard
- 3 tablespoons Worcestershire sauce
- 2 tablespoons mayonnaise
- 2 tablespoons bottled hot sauce, such as Red Rooster
- 2 teaspoons chopped fresh parsley
- 2 teaspoons Old Bay seasoning
- 1 teaspoon cracked white pepper
- 1 teaspoon ground black pepper
- 3 tablespoons olive oil
- 3 tablespoons diced red bell pepper
- 3 tablespoons diced green bell pepper
- 1 cup fine dry bread crumbs
- 1 egg, lightly beaten
- 1 cup panko (Japanese-style bread crumbs*)

1. In a large mixing bowl combine crabmeat, mustard, the Worcestershire sauce, mayonnaise, hot sauce, parsley, Old Bay seasoning, white pepper, and black pepper. Set aside.

2. In a small frying pan heat 1½ tablespoons of the oil over medium heat. Add red and green peppers; cook until they are wilted. Set aside to cool.

3. When peppers are cool, add them to bowl with crabmeat along with ¼ cup of the regular bread crumbs. Stir together. Add egg to crab mixture and combine well. In a shallow dish combine the remaining regular bread crumbs and panko.

4. Shape the crab mixture into 12 round cakes and coat with bread crumb mixture.

5. Heat the remaining 1½ tablespoons olive oil in a skillet over medium-high heat. Fry crab cakes until golden brown on each side and cooked through.

*NOTE: PANKO BREAD CRUMBS ARE USED IN JAPANESE COOKING FOR COATING FRIED FOODS. THEY ARE COARSER THAN TYPICAL DRIED BREAD CRUMBS AND MAKE A VERY CRUNCHY COATING.

# 5 BRAISE 'EM UP

you can't beat braising for meat that's so tender it almost melts off the bone. Yeah, grilling and sautéing are fast, but braising-browning the meat first and then letting it cook long and slow over low heat-gives you awesome flavor, color, and juiciness. (You know what I'm talking about Ö) And while that braised dish is cooking in your oven and filling your home with great smells, you have time to do other things around the house, like setting a beautiful table, decanting some wine, and turning on some smooth tunes.

# braised vegetables with balsamic vinegar

makes 6 servings

4 Japanese eggplants, halved
4 jumbo carrots, peeled and coarsely chopped
8 roma tomatoes, halved
3 small red onions, quartered
2 large zucchini, cut up
2 large yellow summer squash, cut up
6 cloves garlic, smashed
Kosher salt and ground black pepper
1 tablespoon cooking oil
1 cup balsamic vinegar

1. Season the vegetables and garlic with salt and pepper.

2. Heat the oil in a Dutch oven over medium-high heat. Add vegetables; sauté for 3 minutes.

3. Add the vinegar and bring to boiling. Reduce heat; cover, and simmer for 15 minutes or until vegetables are tender.

# prosciutto-wrapped pork tenderloin with braised mushroom ragoût

makes 4 to 6 servings

- 2 pork tenderloins (1 to 1½ pounds, each)
- Kosher salt and ground black pepper
- 2 tablespoons cooking oil
- 12 to 14 slices prosciutto
- ½ cup sliced shiitake mushrooms
- ½ cup sliced oyster mushrooms
- ½ cup sliced morel mushrooms
- 2 tablespoons diced shallots
- 1 tablespoon shaved garlic
- ¼ cup white wine
- 6 tablespoons cold unsalted butter

1. Season the pork with salt and pepper.
2. Heat 1 tablespoon of the oil in a large pan. Add the pork to the pan; sear for 2 minutes on all sides. Remove the pork from the pan and slice into 2-ounce portions. Wrap each portion with a slice of prosciutto, cut to fit. Return the pork to the pan, searing the prosciutto on all sides. Place the pork pieces back in the pan, cut side down; cover and cook for another 5 to 7 minutes or until medium (160°F), turning once.
3. For the ragoût, add the remaining 1 tablespoon oil to a sauté pan. Add all the mushrooms, shallots, and garlic. Season the mixture with salt and pepper and sauté for 3 to 5 minutes or until tender. Add the wine and bring to a boil. Reduce heat and simmer for 3 minutes or until liquid is reduced by half. Whisk in butter, 1 tablespoon at a time. Serve the ragoût with the pork.

NOTE: YOU CAN USE ANY COMBINATION OF WILD AND DOMESTIC MUSHROOMS TO EQUAL 1½ CUPS.

# braised short rib stew with truffle rice

makes 8 servings

- 2 pounds boneless beef short ribs
- Kosher salt and ground black pepper
- Garlic salt
- Seasoned salt
- 2 tablespoons cooking oil
- 4 cups beef stock
- 4 cups chicken stock
- 2 cups chopped onions
- 2 cups chopped carrots
- 2 cups chopped plum tomatoes
- 6 cloves garlic, smashed
- 6 cups hot cooked basmati rice
- 1/4 cup white truffle oil*
- Juice of 1 lemon
- 2 tablespoons unsalted butter
- 1 tablespoon chopped truffles (optional)*
- 1 tablespoon minced garlic

1. Season the short ribs with salt, pepper, garlic salt, and seasoned salt.

2. Preheat oven to 325°F. Heat the oil in a large heavy roasting pan over medium-high heat. Sear the meat for 3 minutes on each side.

3. Add the beef and chicken stocks; bring to boiling. Cover with foil and place in the oven for 1 hour. Add the onions, carrots, tomatoes, and 6 cloves smashed garlic. Cook for 1 hour more; check for tenderness. When the ribs are super tender, remove from pan.

4. For the rice, combine the cooked rice, the truffle oil, and the lemon juice; season with salt and pepper. Add butter, mix well. Stir in the truffles, if using, and minced garlic.

5. Serve short ribs with vegetables and truffled rice; drizzle with cooking juices.

*NOTE: SEE PAGE 75 FOR INFORMATION ON PURCHASING TRUFFLES AND TRUFFLE OIL.

# braised filet mignon with morel mushrooms, pearl onions, and baby carrots

makes 8 servings

- 2 pounds beef tenderloin
- Kosher salt and ground black pepper
- 1 tablespoon cooking oil
- 12 to 14 peeled baby carrots
- 12 to 14 peeled pearl onions
- 2 tablespoons chopped shallots
- 2 tablespoons shaved garlic
- 2 cups red wine
- 2 cups veal stock or beef stock*
- 2 cups morel mushrooms or other wild mushrooms, sliced

1. Season the beef with salt and pepper.
2. Heat oil in a Dutch oven over medium-high heat. Add the beef and sear for 3 to 5 minutes on all sides.
3. Add the carrots, onions, shallots, and garlic to the pan. Cook and stir 2 to 3 minutes or until vegetables begin to soften. Add the wine and the stock; bring to boiling. Reduce heat and simmer for 3 to 5 minutes. Add the mushrooms, cover, and cook for another 25 to 27 minutes for medium (160°F). Remove meat and cover with foil for 10 minutes before slicing. Serve meat with the vegetables.

*NOTE: WHEN USING BEEF STOCK, REMEMBER THAT THE FLAVOR—ESPECIALLY SALT—MAY BE MORE PRONOUNCED WHEN IT IS REDUCED.

# braised lamb with crispy bacon, oyster mushrooms, and fresh rosemary

makes 10 servings

- 3 pounds boneless lamb loin, fat trimmed
- Garlic salt
- Seasoned salt
- Kosher salt and ground black pepper
- 1 tablespoon cooking oil
- 6 strips bacon, chopped
- 8 to 12 cloves garlic, crushed
- 12 to 14 peeled baby carrots
- 2 onions, chopped
- 8 ounces fresh oyster mushrooms
- 1 bunch fresh rosemary sprigs
- 2 cups red wine

1. Season the lamb with garlic salt, seasoned salt, kosher salt and pepper.

2. Heat the oil in a medium heavy roasting pan over medium-high heat. Add the lamb, bacon, and garlic; sear the lamb until browned on all sides and bacon is crisp, 5 to 10 minutes.

3. Add the carrots, onions, mushrooms, rosemary, and wine. Bring to boiling. Reduce heat and simmer, covered, for 10 minutes or until the meat and vegetables are the desired doneness. Remove meat and vegetables from pan. Continue simmering cooking liquid until reduced to desired consistency. Serve cooking liquid with the meat and vegetables.

SERVING SUGGESTION: THIS DISH CAN BE SERVED WITH GARLIC MASHED POTATOES, PAGE 16.

# braised veal loin with trumpet mushrooms

makes 8 to 10 servings

- 2 boneless veal loin roasts (about 3 pounds each)
- Kosher salt and ground black pepper
- 1 tablespoon chopped Italian (flat-leaf) parsley
- 2 teaspoons chopped fresh thyme
- 2 teaspoons chopped fresh rosemary
- 1 tablespoon cooking oil
- 1 cup chopped pancetta
- 2 tablespoons minced garlic
- 2 cups white wine
- 1 cup veal stock or chicken stock
- 2 cups black trumpet or other wild mushrooms, sliced

1. Season the veal with salt and pepper. Sprinkle with the herbs and pat to adhere.

2. Heat the oil in a Dutch oven over medium-high heat. Add the pancetta and the garlic; cook for 2 minutes or until the pancetta begins to get crisp and release fat. Add the veal and sear for 3 to 5 minutes on all sides. Add the wine and the stock. Bring to boiling. Reduce heat and simmer, covered, for 20 minutes. Add the mushrooms. Cover and continue to simmer 10 minutes more until the veal is at medium (160°F). Remove veal from pan, cover loosely with foil and let stand for 10 minutes.

3. To serve, slice the veal into 2-ounce portions and drizzle a small amount of the pancetta jus over the top.

# braised cornish game hens with potatoes and leeks

makes 4 servings

- 4 Cornish game hens, cut into quarters
- Kosher salt and ground black pepper
- 1 tablespoon cooking oil
- 4 russet potatoes, peeled and chopped
- 2 large leeks, white parts only, coarsely chopped
- 6 cloves garlic, smashed
- 2 cups peeled and chopped plum tomatoes
- 2 cups white wine
- 2 cups chicken stock or broth

1. Season the hens with salt and pepper.

2. Heat the oil in a large heavy roasting pan over medium-high heat. Add the hens to the oil and sear on all sides. Add the potatoes, leeks, and garlic; sauté for 3 minutes, or until leeks are tender. Add the tomatoes, wine, and stock. Bring to boiling. Reduce heat, cover, and let simmer for 25 to 30 minutes on low heat or until hens and potatoes are tender. Serve hens with vegetables and sauce.

"CORNISH GAME HEN IS SURPRISINGLY TASTY AND QUICK TO COOK. TRUST ME, YOU'RE GONNA LOVE THIS ONE."

# braised quail with pancetta, dried cranberries, and shiitake mushrooms

makes 6 appetizer servings

- 6 whole quail, cut into quarters
- Kosher salt and ground black pepper
- 1 tablespoon cooking oil
- 2 cups diced pancetta
- 1/2 pound fresh shiitake mushrooms, coarsely chopped
- 1 cup dried cranberries
- 3 tablespoons shaved garlic
- 2 cups port wine
- 1 cup chicken stock
- 3 tablespoons unsalted butter
- Green Oil (see recipe, page 15)
- Hot cooked basmati or brown rice
- Thyme sprigs (optional)

1. Season quail with salt and pepper.

2. Heat the oil in a Dutch oven. Add the quail; sear on all sides. Add the pancetta, mushrooms, cranberries, and garlic. Continue cooking until pancetta is crisp and mushrooms are tender. Add the wine and stock; bring to boiling. Reduce heat and simmer, covered, for 15 to 20 minutes or until quail are tender. Remove quail from the pan. Simmer cooking liquid, uncovered, 10 minutes or until the cooking liquid is thickened. Whisk in butter.

3. Place quail on a serving plate. Drizzle with some of the cooking liquid, mushrooms, cranberries, and a few pieces of pancetta. Drizzle the plate with Green Oil. Serve with rice and thyme sprigs, if desired.

# braised garlic and sage chicken

makes 4 servings

- 8 chicken thighs, skin on
- Kosher salt and ground black pepper
- 1 tablespoon cooking oil
- 8 medium red bee potatoes or other round red potatoes, halved
- 2 medium onions, coarsely chopped
- 1 bunch fresh sage, leaves picked from the stems
- 1 tablespoon chopped fresh rosemary
- 6 cloves garlic, smashed
- 2 cups white wine
- 2 cups veal stock or chicken stock
- 3 tablespoons unsalted butter

1. Season the chicken with salt and pepper.

2. Heat the oil in a heavy roasting pan over medium-high heat. Place the chicken in the hot oil, skin side down, and sear the skin. Turn the chicken and add the potatoes, onions, herbs, and garlic; sauté for 3 minutes or until vegetables begin to soften. Add the wine and stock. Bring to boiling. Reduce heat, cover and simmer on low to medium heat for 25 to 30 minutes or until chicken and vegetables are tender. Stir in butter.

# 6 SOMETIMES I GRILL

I've always loved *working on the grill. There's just something about charring a steak, splitting an Italian sausage, or getting those grill marks on a thick piece of salmon. Nowadays I have my grill guys-my cousin Stanley, Darrin King (aka Big D), and my brother-in-law Kevin (who thinks he can out-grill me). They love the grill so much they set it right outside the living room door so we can still watch the game and the flames while having cold ones. It's kinda like the old saying: When boy meets grill, it's time to chill!*

# marinated t-bone steak

makes 8 servings

- 1 cup A-1® steak sauce
- 1 cup Bulls-Eye barbecue sauce
- 1 tablespoon Worcestershire sauce
- 1/4 cup chopped fresh rosemary
- 1/4 cup chopped fresh thyme
- 3 tablespoons minced garlic
- 2 tablespoons diced shallots
- 2 tablespoons light brown sugar
- 1 tablespoon cracked black pepper
- 8 8-ounce beef T-bone steaks

1. For the marinade, in a large bowl combine steak sauce, barbecue sauce, and Worcestershire sauce. Stir in rosemary, thyme, garlic, shallots, brown sugar, and pepper.

2. Place the steaks in a resealable bag set in a shallow bowl. Pour the marinade over the steaks. Seal bag. Marinate in the refrigerator for 2 hours, turning occasaionally.

3. Drain steaks; discard marinade. Place the steaks on the rack of an uncovered grill directly over medium coals. Grill 10 to 13 minutes for medium-rare (145°F) or 12 to 15 minutes for medium (160°F), turning once.

GRILLED BLACK PEPPER AND SEA SALT-CRUSTED COWBOY RIBEYE STEAK, PAGE 142

SEASONED FILET MIGNON WITH WHOLE GARLIC, PAGE 143

# grilled black pepper and sea salt-crusted cowboy ribeye steak

makes 4 servings

- 2 cups olive oil
- 2 cups A-1® steak sauce
- 2 large onions, coarsely chopped
- 1 bunch fresh rosemary sprigs
- 1 bunch fresh thyme sprigs
- 10 cloves garlic, smashed
- 2 18-ounce beef ribeye steaks
- 1/4 cup sea salt
- 1/4 cup coarsely ground black pepper

1. For the marinade, in a large bowl combine the oil, steak sauce, onions, rosemary, thyme, and garlic.

2. Place the steaks in a resealable bag set in a shallow bowl. Pour marinade over the steaks. Seal bag. Marinate in the refrigerator for 24 hours, turning occasionally.

3. Drain steaks; discard the marinade. Generously season the steaks with the sea salt and the coarse black pepper.

4. Preheat a grill. Place steaks on the rack of an uncovered grill directly over medium coals. Grill for 15 to 19 minutes for medium-rare (145°F) or 18 to 23 minutes for medium (160°F), turning once.

# seasoned filet mignon with whole garlic

makes 12 servings

1 4-pound center cut beef tenderloin roast
8 cloves peeled garlic
2 tablespoons olive oil
1 tablespoon seasoned salt
Kosher salt and ground black pepper

1. Using a small paring knife, cut eight very small slits in the tenderloin just wide enough to slide one clove of garlic into each slit.

2. Rub the meat with the oil then season the whole tenderloin with the seasoned salt, kosher salt, and pepper. Use 100 percent cotton kitchen string to tie the roast at 2-inch intervals for even cooking.

3. Arrange hot coals around a drip pan. Test for medium-high heat above the pan. Place tenderloin roast on a grill rack over the drip pan. Cover; grill for 1 to 1¼ hours or until an instant-read thermometer inserted into the thickest part of the roast reads 135°F for medium rare. Remove meat from the grill. Cover with foil and let stand for 15 minutes. Remove string; slice and serve.

“IN THE GREAT WORDS OF JAMES BROWN, 'THIS IS A MAN'S WORLD'–BUT WHEN IT COMES TO A GREAT STEAK LIKE THIS, I THINK WE HAVE TO SHARE ...”

# grilled balsamic marinated flank steak

makes 12 servings

- 1 cup balsamic vinegar
- 1/4 cup Dijon mustard
- 1/4 cup packed light brown sugar
- 1 tablespoon chopped fresh rosemary
- 1 tablespoon chopped fresh thyme
- 6 cloves garlic, smashed
- 1 cup olive oil
- 3 pounds beef flank steak (2 steaks)
- Kosher salt and ground black pepper

1. For the marinade, in a large bowl combine the vinegar, mustard, brown sugar, rosemary, thyme, and garlic; mix well. Slowly pour in the oil, while whisking constantly.

2. Place the steaks in a resealable bag set in a shallow bowl. Pour the marinade over the steak. Seal bag. Marinate in the refrigerator for 24 hours, turning occasionally.

3. Drain steaks, reserving marinade. Season steaks with salt and pepper. Place steaks on the rack of an uncovered grill directly over medium coals. Grill for 17 to 21 minutes for medium (160°F), turning once and frequently brushing more marinade on the meat as it cooks.

# onion-marinated new york steak

makes 6 servings

- 1 bunch fresh thyme sprigs
- 1 bunch fresh rosemary sprigs
- 12 cloves garlic, smashed
- 2 tablespoons green peppercorns
- 2 cups olive oil
- 2 cups A-1® steak sauce
- 2 medium onions, coarsely chopped
- 1/4 cup coarse sea salt
- 1 teaspoon crushed red pepper
- 6 8-ounce beef New York strip (top loin) steaks

1. For the marinade, in a large bowl combine the thyme and rosemary sprigs, garlic, and peppercorns. Add the oil, steak sauce, onions, salt, and the crushed red pepper; mix well.

2. Place the steaks in a resealable bag set in a shallow bowl. Pour marinade over the steaks. Seal bag. Marinate in refrigerator for 2 hours, turning occasionally.

3. Drain steaks, discarding marinade. Place steaks on the rack of an uncovered grill directly over medium coals. Grill 10 to 12 minutes for medium-rare (145°F) or 12 to 15 minutes for medium (160°F), turning once.

NOTE: BE SURE WHEN YOU MARINATE YOUR STEAKS THAT YOU DON'T ADD TOO MUCH SALT TO THE MARINADE. IT WILL PULL MOISTURE FROM THE MEAT. SEASON YOUR STEAKS WITH SALT JUST BEFORE COOKING.

# kicked-up burgers

makes 3 servings

- 1 pound ground beef
- 3 tablespoons Worcestershire sauce
- 2 teaspoons chopped garlic
- 2 teaspoons chopped shallot
- 2 teaspoons chopped fresh Italian (flat leaf) parsley
- 1/4 teaspoon salt
- Pinch cayenne pepper
- 1 egg, lightly beaten
- 1 teaspoon black pepper
- 2 tablespoons bread crumbs
- 5 tablespoons olive oil
- 3 sourdough hamburger buns
- 3 tablespoons mayonnaise
- 3 teaspoons Dijon mustard
- Pinch ground black pepper

1. In a large glass bowl combine ground beef, Worcestershire sauce, garlic, shallot, parsley, salt, and cayenne pepper. Add egg and the 1 teaspoon black pepper; mix well. Add bread crumbs and mix again. Roll one-third of meat mixture into a ball and pat it down into a patty. Repeat to make two more patties.

2. In a sauté pan heat olive oil over medium-high heat. Add patties to pan. When one side is cooked halfway through, flip the burgers so the other side can cook.

3. Open 3 sourdough buns and spread 1 tablespoon mayonnaise and 1 teaspoon mustard on each bun. Sprinkle with a pinch of black pepper. Place a burger on the bottom of each bun. Add desired burger toppings and the top of the bun.

# grilled honey-orange-marinated pork tenderloin

makes 4 servings

- 2 pork tenderloins
- 2 cups honey
- 1/4 cup chopped fresh cilantro
- 1/4 cup chopped fresh rosemary
- 1/4 cup chopped fresh thyme
- 2 tablespoons light brown sugar
- 2 tablespoons minced garlic
- 1 tablespoon Dijon mustard
- 1 cup fresh orange juice
- 1 cup apple juice
- 1/4 cup olive oil
- 2 tablespoons soy sauce

1. Trim the excess fat from the pork tenderloins, or have the butcher do it for you.

2. For the marinade, in a large bowl combine the honey, cilantro, rosemary, thyme, brown sugar, garlic, and mustard. Add the orange and apple juices, oil, and soy sauce; mix well.

3. Place the pork in a resealable bag set in a shallow bowl. Pour the marinade over the pork. Seal bag. Marinate in refrigerator for 2 hours, turning occasionally.

4. Drain pork; discard marinade. Place medium-hot coals around a drip pan. Test for medium heat above the pan. Place the pork on the grill rack over the drip pan. Cover and grill for 30 to 35 minutes for medium (160°F). Remove pork from grill. Cover pork with foil. Let stand for 10 minutes. Slice and serve.

# grilled pork chops with warm apple butter

makes 6 servings

- 6 12-ounce bone-in pork rib chops
- 2 tablespoons olive oil
- Kosher salt and ground black pepper
- 4 Granny Smith apples
- 1/2 cup cognac
- 1/4 cup raisins
- 2 tablespoons brown sugar
- 1 stick cinnamon
- 3 tablespoons unsalted butter
- 1 teaspoon balsamic vinegar

1. Brush the chops with 1 tablespoon of the oil and season with salt and pepper.

2. Place chops on an uncovered grill rack directly over medium coals. Grill 16 to 20 minutes or until an instant-read thermometer inserted into the thickest part of the meat reads 160°F, turning once.

3. While the chops are cooking, peel and chop the apples. In a sauté pan heat the remaining 1 tablespoon oil over medium heat. Add the apples and sauté for 5 minutes, or until tender. Remove from the heat. Carefully add the cognac, raisins, brown sugar, and cinnamon. Return to heat and bring to a boil. Reduce heat and simmer until the alcohol burns off and liquid is reduced to desired consistency. Remove cinnamon stick. Add the butter and the balsamic vinegar.

4. Place the chops on a serving plate. Spoon the apple butter mixture over the chops. Sprinkle with additional ground black pepper.

# garlic-rosemary colorado lamb loin

makes 6 to 8 servings

- 2 cups honey
- 2 cups olive oil
- 6 cloves garlic, crushed
- 1 tablespoon chopped fresh rosemary
- 1 2- to 3-pound boneless Colorado lamb loin roast (double loin, tied)
- Kosher salt and ground black pepper
- Rosemary Potatoes and Carrots (see recipe, below )

1. For the marinade, in a large bowl whisk together the honey, oil, garlic, and rosemary.

2. Place the lamb in a resealable bag set in a shallow bowl. Pour marinade over meat. Seal bag. Marinate in the refrigerator for 4 hours, turning occasionally.

3. Drain lamb; discard marinade. Season meat with salt and pepper. Place medium-hot coals around a drip pan. Test for medium heat above pan. Place lamb on the grill rack over drip pan. Cover and grill for 45 minutes to 1 hour or until an instant-read thermometer inserted in the thickest part of the roast reads 135°F. Remove meat from the grill. Cover meat with foil; let stand for 15 minutes.

4. To serve, slice lamb and serve with Rosemary Potatoes and Carrots.

ROSEMARY POTATOES AND CARROTS

Preheat oven to 350°F. Place 5 quartered small red potatoes and 2 cups peeled baby carrots in a baking dish. Add 1 tablespoon each: chopped garlic, chopped shallot, chopped fresh rosemary, and chopped fresh thyme. Dot vegetables with 3 tablespoons butter. Bake in oven for 20 to 30 minutes or until vegetables are tender.

# 5-spice-marinated herbed chicken

makes 6 servings

- 1/4 cup seasoned salt
- 1/4 cup garlic salt
- 1/4 cup onion powder
- 1/4 cup barbecue spice blend
- 3 tablespoons minced garlic
- 2 tablespoons chopped fresh rosemary
- 2 tablespoons chopped fresh thyme
- 1 tablespoon ground white pepper
- 1 cup olive oil-canola oil blend or olive oil
- 12 meaty chicken pieces (asssortment of thighs, breasts, legs)

1. In a large bowl combine seasoned salt, garlic salt, onion powder, barbecue spice blend, garlic, rosemary, thyme, and white pepper; mix well. Slowly add the oil until it makes a light paste (you may not need all of the oil).

2. Rub each piece of chicken with the paste and place the chicken in a resealable bag set in a shallow bowl. Add remaining paste to the bag. Seal bag. Marinate in refrigerator for 2 hours.

3. Remove chicken from bag. Remove and discard excess paste. Place chicken on the rack of an uncovered grill directly over medium coals. Grill for 35 to 45 minutes or until an instant-read thermometer inserted into the meaty portion of a thigh piece registers 180°F, turning once.

“THE FIVE SPICES IN THIS RECIPE MAKE THE CHICKEN TASTE OVER THE TOP—WHITE MEAT OR DARK MEAT WORKS HERE. TAKE YOUR PICK.”

# balsamic-glazed grilled cornish game hens

makes 4 servings

- 1 cup olive oil
- 2 tablespoons chopped fresh rosemary
- 2 tablespoons chopped fresh thyme
- 2 tablespoons minced garlic
- 4 Cornish game hens
- Kosher salt and ground black pepper
- 1 cup Balsamic Reduction (see recipe, page 15)

1. For the marinade, in a medium bowl combine the oil, rosemary, thyme, and garlic.

2. Using a long heavy knife or kitchen shears, halve the Cornish game hens lengthwise, cutting through the breast bone, just off-center, and through the center of the backbone. Twist wing tips under back. Place the hens in a resealable bag set in a shallow bowl. Pour marinade over the hens. Seal bag. Marinate in the refrigerator for 4 hours, turning occasionally.

3. Drain hens; discard marinade. Season the hens with salt and pepper. Arrange medium-hot coals around a drip pan. Test for medium heat above the pan. Place hens, bone sides down, on rack over drip pan. Cover; grill for 30 minutes. Brush the hens all over with the balsamic reduction. Grill for another 5 to 8 minutes, watching closely, just until the reduction makes a nice glaze and an instant-read thermometer inserted into a thigh registers 180°F.

# grilled jumbo shrimp with prosciutto and asparagus

makes 12 appetizer or 6 main dish servings

24 pencil-thin asparagus spears
12 jumbo shrimp, peeled and deveined
1 tablespoon canola oil
Kosher salt and ground black pepper
12 slices prosciutto

1. Cook asparagus, covered, in a small amount of boiling salted water for 3 minutes. Drain. Immediately place in a bowl of ice water to stop cooking. Drain again. Pat dry with paper towels; set aside.

2. Brush the shrimp lightly with oil, then season with salt and pepper.

3. Place the shrimp on the rack of an uncovered grill directly over medium coals. Grill shrimp for 2 minutes, turning once. Remove the shrimp from the grill and set aside for 5 minutes to cool.

4. When the shrimp have cooled, wrap two asparagus spears and one shrimp in a slice of prosciutto. Repeat with remaining asparagus, shrimp, and prosciutto.

5. Place wrapped shrimp back on the grill. Grill for 4 to 7 minutes more or until the shrimp is opaque, turning occasionally so the prosciutto doesn't burn. Sprinkle with additional ground black pepper.

# grilled orange-glazed shrimp

makes 4 servings

- 12 jumbo shrimp, peeled and deveined
- Kosher salt and ground black pepper
- 1 tablespoon olive oil
- 1/3 cup sour cream
- 1/3 cup orange juice
- 3 tablespoons mayonnaise
- 1 1/2 teaspoons sugar
- 1/2 teaspoon lemon juice (optional)

1. Season the shrimp with salt and pepper and drizzle with the oil.

2. Place the shrimp on the rack of an uncovered grill directly over medium coals. Grill for 7 to 9 minutes or until opaque, turning once.

3. In a large bowl combine the sour cream, orange juice, mayonnaise, and sugar. Mix well and season to taste with salt and pepper, and lemon juice, if desired. Toss the shrimp into the sauce and serve.

SAUTÉED ORANGE-GLAZED SHRIMP

Season the peeled and deveined shrimp with salt and pepper. In a medium bowl toss shrimp in 2 tablespoons all-purpose flour. In a sauté pan, heat 1 tablespoon olive oil and 1 tablespoon butter over medium heat. Sauté the shrimp until the shrimp turn opaque. Prepare orange glaze as above. Toss the shrimp in the sauce to serve.

# bbq grilled scallop and salmon skewers

makes 3 servings

- 9 large sea scallops
- 9 ounces salmon, without skin, cut into 1-ounce portions
- Kosher salt and ground black pepper
- 1 tablespoon olive oil
- 1/2 cup Bulls-Eye® barbecue sauce

1. Alternate three scallops and three salmon portions on three 12- to 14-inch metal skewers. Season the fish with salt and pepper and drizzle with oil.

2. Place the skewers on the greased grill rack of an uncovered grill directly over medium coals. Grill for 8 minutes, turning once.

3. Brush the skewers on both sides with the barbecue sauce and grill for another 3 to 5 minutes or until scallops are opaque and the salmon flakes easily when tested with a fork.

# 7 GOURMET SANDWICHES

**mom set some** simple rules for my siblings and me while we were growing up: Get home from school, do your homework, clean your room, and start dinner. Most days that plan worked fine, but there were times when none of us wanted to cook. We didn't want to get in trouble, so we all decided to make sandwiches. "OK, if that's what y'all want," Mom would say. And so my love for sandwiches was born! Even today, with a kitchen of cool tools and a fridge full of gourmet ingredients, there's nothing like a meal of fresh cold cuts and cheese, homebaked bread, and real mayo made at home.

# corned beef
## with provolone

makes 1 sandwich

- 1 tablespoon melted butter
- 2 slices fresh ciabatta bread
- 2 tablespoons Dijon and Garlic Aïoli (see recipe, page 165)
- 4 ounces sliced corned beef
- 2 tablespoons Sautéed Onions (see recipe, below)
- 2 slices provolone cheese
- 2 leaves butterhead lettuce

1. Spread a little butter on each side of the bread. Place bread on the rack of an uncovered grill directly over medium coals for 1 to 2 minutes for a light toasting. Or place on a hot grill pan until bread is toasted.

2. Spread some Dijon and Garlic Aïoli on one side of the bread. Lay the corned beef on one bread slice and top with Sautéed Onions, the cheese, then the lettuce. Place the other bread slice on top and slice.

SAUTÉED ONIONS: SLICE ONE ONION VERY THINLY. HEAT A SMALL AMOUNT OF OLIVE OIL IN A SAUTÉ PAN OVER MEDIUM-HIGH HEAT. ADD ONION SLICES; SAUTÉ FOR 5 TO 7 MINUTES OR UNTIL ONIONS ARE TENDER AND SLIGHTLY CARAMEL IN COLOR.

# roast beef with sun-dried tomatoes and sautéed onions

makes 1 sandwich

- 2 slices sourdough bread
- 1½ tablespoons sour cream
- 1 tablespoon grated fresh horseradish
- ½ teaspoon minced garlic
- ½ teaspoon lemon juice
- Kosher salt and ground black pepper
- 3 ounces sliced roast beef, warm or cold
- 1 tablespoon oil-packed sun-dried tomatoes, drained and cut in strips
- 2 tablespoons Sautéed Onions (see recipe, page 161)
- 4 leaves arugula

1. Toast the bread on a hot grill pan or in a 350°F oven for 8 minutes or until brown.

2. In a small bowl combine the sour cream, horseradish, garlic, and lemon juice. Mix well and season to taste with salt and pepper; refrigerate until ready to use.

3. Spread the horseradish sauce on one side of the bread slices. Place the roast beef on one bread slice; put the sun-dried tomatoes, the Sautéed Onions and arugula on top of the onions. Top with remaining bread slice.

## white truffle and pepper

makes 1¼ cups

- 2 large egg yolks
- 1 tablespoon white vinegar
- 1 cup canola oil
- 2 tablespoons white truffle oil
- 1 pinch ground white pepper
- Kosher salt

1. Combine egg yolks and vinegar in a blender. Cover and blend on low speed.
2. With the blender running on slow speed, slowly pour in the canola oil and the white truffle oil until the aïoli is combined and thickened like mayonnaise.
3. Stir in the white pepper. Season to taste with salt.

## basil aïoli

makes 1¼ cups

- 2 large egg yolks
- 1 tablespoon lemon juice
- ¾ cup canola oil
- ¼ cup Green Oil (see recipe, page 15)
- 2 tablespoons chopped basil
- Kosher salt and ground black pepper

1. Combine the egg yolks and lemon juice in a blender. Cover and blend on low speed.
2. With the blender running on slow speed, slowly pour in the canola oil and the Green Oil until the aïoli is combined and thickened like mayonnaise.
3. Fold in the basil and season to taste with salt and pepper.

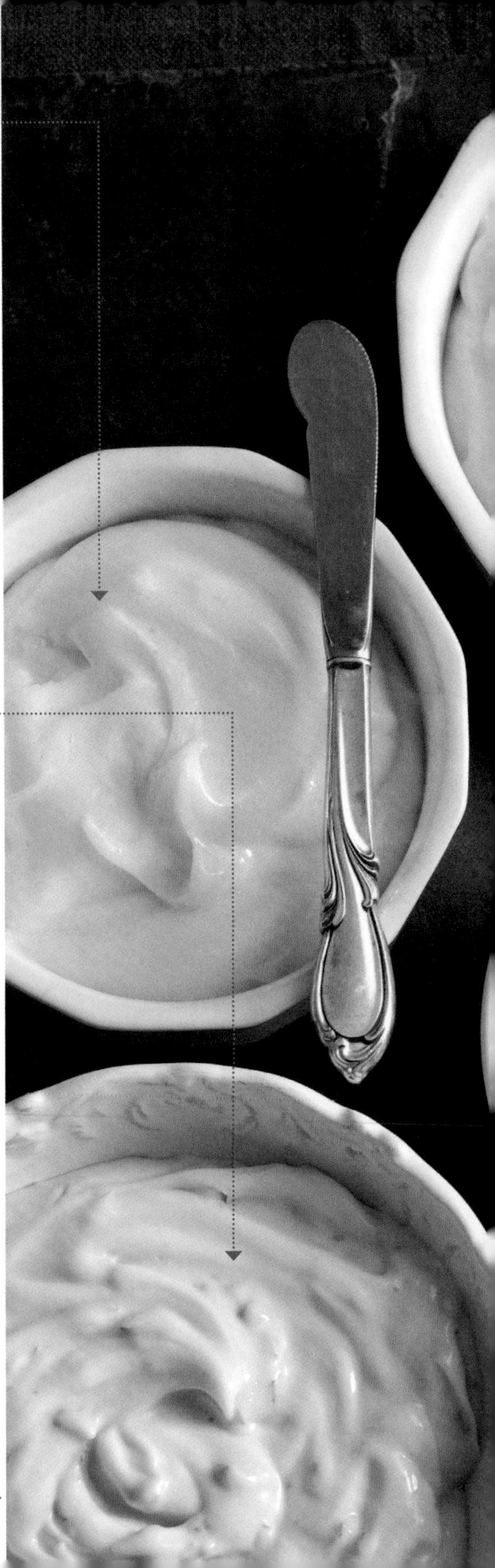

## dijon and garlic aïoli

makes 1¼ cups

- 2 large egg yolks
- 1 tablespoon lemon juice
- 2 tablespoons Dijon mustard
- 1 tablespoon minced garlic
- 1 cup canola oil
- 3 tablespoons chopped fresh chives
- Kosher salt and ground black pepper

1. Combine the egg yolks, lemon juice, and mustard in a blender. Cover and blend on low speed.

2. With the blender running on slow speed, add the garlic, and slowly pour in the oil until the aïoli is combined and thickened like mayonnaise.

3. Fold in the chives and season to taste with salt and pepper.

## chile and garlic aïoli

makes 1¼ cups

- 2 large egg yolks
- 1 tablespoon lemon juice
- 1 cup canola oil
- 1 chipotle chile pepper in adobo sauce, chopped
- 2 teaspoons adobo sauce (from the can of chipotles)
- 1 teaspoon minced garlic
- Kosher salt and ground black pepper

1. Combine egg yolks and lemon juice in a blender. Cover and blend on low speed.

2. With the motor running on slow speed, slowly pour in the oil until the aioli is combined and thickened like mayonnaise.

3. Stir in chipotle, adobo sauce, and garlic. Season to taste with salt and pepper.

# grilled **chicken breast** with crispy prosciutto, arugula and avocado

makes 1 sandwich

- 1 slice prosciutto
- 2 tablespoons Chile and Garlic Aïoli (see recipe, page 165)
- 1 piece focaccia bread, split horizontally
- 4 ounces grilled skinless boneless chicken breast, bias-sliced
- 1/4 of an avocado, sliced
- 5 leaves arugula
- 2 slices Gruyère cheese

1. Preheat oven to 400°F. Place the prosciutto on a baking pan; bake for 4 to 6 minutes or until crispy.

2. Spread the aïoli on the cut surfaces of the bread. Place the chicken on one bread piece, then add the avocado, the prosciutto, the arugula, and the cheese. Place the other half of the bread on top and serve.

NOTE: IF YOU LIKE, PLACE THE SANDWICHES ON A BAKING SHEET AND LIGHTLY TOAST FOR 3 TO 5 MINUTES OR UNTIL THE CHEESE IS MELTED.

# warm BLT with chicken

makes 1 sandwich

1 4-inch piece ciabatta bread, split horizontally
3 tablespoons Basil Aïoli (see recipe, page 164)
4 ounces grilled skinless boneless chicken breast, bias-sliced
3 leaves butterleaf lettuce
2 strips bacon, crisp-cooked
4 slices vine-ripened tomatoes

1. Grill the bread, cut side down, on the grill rack of an uncovered grill directly over medium coals for 1 to 2 minutes or until toasted. Or preheat a grill pan and grill bread for 1 to 2 minutes or until toasted.

2. Spread the aïoli on one side of each piece of bread. Add the chicken breast, lettuce, bacon, and tomato. Top with second piece of bread.

NOTE: IF YOU LIKE, ADD TWO SLICES OF YOUR FAVORITE CHEESE. THE CHICKEN CAN ALSO BE SAUTÉED, IF YOU PREFER.

# grilled andouille sausage with prosciutto, sun-dried tomatoes, and gruyère

makes 6 sandwiches

- 2 tablespoons olive oil
- 1 cup thinly sliced shallots
- 6 andouille sausage links
- 6 thin slices of proscuitto
- 1/4 cup Dijon and Garlic Aïoli (see recipe, page 165)
- 6 good quality hot dog buns, toasted
- 6 slices Gruyère cheese
- 1 cup oil-packed sun-dried tomatoes, drained and cut in thin strips

1. Preheat your grill, or if using a grill pan, place it over medium-high heat. Heat the oil in a sauté pan over medium-high heat. Sauté the shallots until golden. Remove from the pan and keep warm.

2. Place the sausages on the greased rack of an uncovered grill directly over medium coals, rotating them for 6 to 8 minutes until cooked through. Remove from the grill, and wrap each sausage with one slice of proscuitto. Return the sausages to the grill, and warm them over indirect heat about 45 seconds. Remove to a platter and keep warm.

3. Spread the aïoli on the insides of each bun. Top with cheese, sausage, tomatoes, and shallots.

NOTE: IF YOU DON'T HAVE A GRILL OR GRILL PAN, YOU CAN BROIL THE SAUSAGE. FEEL FREE TO GET CREATIVE WITH YOUR DOGS. IF YOU WANT TO CHANGE THE CHEESE OR USE SAUTÉED ONIONS THAT'S OK TOO.

# pan-fried whitefish with vine ripened tomatoes

makes 2 sandwiches

- 2 6-ounce whitefish fillets, skin on, bones removed
- Kosher salt and ground black pepper
- 1/2 cup all-purpose flour
- 1 tablespoon cooking oil
- 1 tablespoon Spanish capers
- 2 tablespoons Basil Aïoli (see recipe, page 164)
- 2 6-inch French baguettes, split horizontally
- 1/2 of a lemon
- 6 leaves butterhead lettuce
- 6 slices vine-ripened tomatoes

1. Season the whitefish with salt and pepper. Place the flour in a shallow dish. Dredge the fish in the flour and pat off the excess.

2. Heat the oil in a sauté pan. Once the oil is hot, place the fish in the oil, skin side down, and sauté for 4 to 6 minutes per 1/2-inch thickness of fish or until fish is crisp and flakes easily when tested with a fork, turning once. Place the fish on a paper towel to drain.

3. Mix the capers into the Basil Aïoli. Spread aïoli on the inside of the baguettes. Squeeze a small amount of juice from the lemon half over the fish. Place a piece of fish on the bottom half of each baguette. Add the lettuce, tomatoes, and baguette tops.

SERVING SUGGESTION: KETTLE CHIPS ARE A PERFECT SIDE FOR THIS CRISPY FISH SANDWICH.

# grilled veggie sandwich

makes 4 sandwiches

- 2 Japanese eggplants, split lengthwise
- 2 zucchini, split lengthwise
- 2 yellow summer squash, split lengthwise
- 1 red sweet pepper, seeded and cut in quarters
- 1 yellow sweet pepper, seeded and cut in quarters
- 2 portobello mushrooms, cleaned and stems removed
- Kosher salt and ground black pepper
- 1 tablespoon olive oil
- 8 slices bread, toasted
- 1/2 cup desired flavor aïoli (see recipes, pages 164-165)
- 1 cup arugula leaves

1. In large bowl combine the eggplant, zucchini, yellow summer squash, sweet peppers, and mushrooms. Season the vegetables with salt and pepper, drizzle with oil; toss to coat.

2. Place vegetables on an uncovered grill directly over medium coals. Grill for 8 minutes or until tender and lightly charred, turning once. Slice vegetables.

3. Spread one side of the bread slices with aïoli. Place the vegetables and arugula on half of the bread slices. Top with remaining bread slices; slice and serve.

“NOW YOU CAN HAVE A PERFECT SANDWICH WITHOUT THE WORRY OF WHAT COLD CUTS YOU WANT TO USE. PICK YOUR FAVORITE VEGGIES–YOU'LL NEVER MISS THE MEAT.”

PAN-FRIED RED SNAPPER
WITH BASIL AÏOLI
SEARED SEA BASS SANDWICH
WITH DIJON AND GARLIC AÏOLI

# pan-fried red snapper with basil aïoli

makes 1 sandwich

- 1 6-ounce portion red snapper or whitefish, skin and pin bones removed
- Kosher salt and ground black pepper
- 1 tablespoon cooking oil
- 1/4 cup all-purpose flour
- 2 tablespoons Basil Aïoli (see recipe, page 164)
- 1 6-inch hoagie roll, split
- 1/2 of a lemon
- 4 slices vine-ripened tomatoes
- 2 leaves butterleaf lettuce

1. Season the fish with salt and pepper.

2. Heat the oil in a sauté pan. Meanwhile, place flour in a shallow dish. Dredge fish in flour and pat off the excess. When the oil is hot, sauté the fish for 4 to 6 minutes per 1/2-inch thickness of fish, or until the fish flakes when tested with a fork, turning once. Remove from pan; place on a paper towel to drain.

3. Spread the aïoli on the cut surfaces of the hoagie. Place the fish on the roll bottom, squeeze a bit of juice from the lemon half over the fish, then add the tomatoes and lettuce. Add roll top and slice.

# seared sea bass sandwich with dijon and garlic aïoli

makes 4 sandwiches

- 8 slices prosciutto (optional)
- 4 6-ounce portions of Chilean sea bass
- Kosher salt and ground black pepper
- 2 tablespoons olive oil
- 2 tablespoons unsalted butter
- 8 slices grilled sourdough bread
- 1/2 cup Dijon and Garlic Aïoli (see recipe, page 165)
- 12 ounces shredded romaine lettuce
- 12 slices vine-ripened tomatoes

1. If using prosciutto, preheat oven to 350°F. Season the fish with salt and pepper. Heat oil and 1 tablespoon of the butter in a sauté pan over medium-high heat. Saute fish for 3 to 4 minutes per side. Remove from heat.

2. If desired, place the slices of proscuitto on a parchment-lined baking sheet; bake until crispy, about 5 minutes. Spread the remaining tablespoon of butter on bread and toast lightly in a grill pan over medium heat.

3. Spread each piece of bread with desired amount of aïoli. Top four slices of the bread with the fish, the lettuce, tomato, and the crispy prosciutto, if using. Top with the remaining slices of bread.

# smoked salmon with fluffy eggs and red onions on focaccia

makes 1 sandwich

- 2 tablespoons sour cream
- 1 teaspoon minced garlic
- 1 tablespoon prepared horseradish
- 1 teaspoon lemon juice
- Kosher salt and ground black pepper
- 2 large organic eggs
- 1 tablespoon whole milk
- 1 tablespoon unsalted butter
- 1 piece focaccia bread
- 3 ounces Norwegian smoked salmon or other lox-style salmon
- Fresh dill, coarsely chopped
- 1 thin slice red onion, separated into rings

1. In a small bowl combine the sour cream, garlic, horseradish, and lemon juice. Mix well and season to taste with salt and pepper; refrigerate spread until ready to use.

2. Break the eggs into a small bowl, add the milk and mix well.

3. In a small sauté pan melt butter over medium heat. Add the egg mixture. Cook without stirring until eggs begin to set on the bottom and sides. With a spatula, lift and fold the partly cooked mixture so the uncooked part moves to the bottom of the pan. Continue cooking and folding until the mixture is cooked through but still looks moist. Season with salt and pepper and remove from the heat.

4. Spread the cut side of each bread piece with the horseradish sauce. Top one cut surface with the scrambled eggs, smoked salmon, dill, and red onion. Top with remaining bread piece.

# 8
# JUST THAT—DESSERTS

## it's simple

You deserve dessert. And don't let anyone talk you out of having it! People often forget that dessert is part of the meal–it's not an option. Here's how I see it: Spend the time to make something great and you'll feel great about eating it. So pour some port, Bailey's, or cognac and enjoy something sweet. Your final course can be a simple brownie or a showy layer cake, but don't let this special part of the evening slip away–and that's that!

# fresh berry trifle

makes 10 to 12 servings

- 1 cup water
- 2 cups sugar
- 1 pint raspberries
- 1 pint blackberries
- 1 pint blueberries
- 1 pint strawberries, sliced
- 4 cups whipping cream
- 1 cup rum, brandy, or framboise
- 1 10¾-ounce fresh or frozen pound cake, thawed and cut into ½-inch slices
- 1 3-ounce bar dark chocolate

1. In a medium saucepan combine the water with 1 cup of the sugar. Bring to boiling, stirring to dissolve sugar. Remove from the heat and set the syrup aside to cool.

2. In a small bowl toss the raspberries with 2 tablespoons of the remaining sugar. In separate bowls, do the same with the blackberries, blueberries, and strawberries; set aside.

3. In a large mixing bowl beat the cream and the remaining ½ cup sugar with an electric mixer until soft peaks form.

4. Combine the simple syrup with the rum, brandy, or framboise.

5. To assemble: Place the blackberries in the bottom of a glass trifle bowl. Arrange sliced pound cake over the berries, then brush the cake with the simple syrup mixture. Spoon some whipped cream on top of the cake. Sprinkle the raspberries on top of the whipped cream followed by another layer of sliced cake. Brush with simple syrup mixture. Spoon more whipped cream on top of the cake. Sprinkle the blueberries on top of the whipped cream. Top with sliced pound cake. Brush with the simple syrup mixture and top cake with the remaining whipped cream. Arrange the sliced strawberries on top of the whipped cream. Using a vegetable peeler, shave the chocolate bar and sprinkle the chocolate shavings on top.

# lemon-raspberry meringue

makes 4 servings

- 2 eggs
- 2 egg yolks
- 2 tablespoons finely shredded lemon peel
- 1/2 cup lemon juice
- 1 1/2 cups sugar
- 1/2 cup unsalted butter, cubed
- 1 10 3/4-ounce fresh or frozen pound cake, thawed and cut into 1/2-inch slices
- 1 pint fresh raspberries
- 4 egg whites

1. In a stainless steel mixing bowl or double boiler, combine whole eggs, egg yolks, lemon peel, lemon juice, and 1/2 cup of the sugar, whisking to incorporate.

2. Put the bowl or double boiler over saucepan of simmering water on medium heat. Whisk mixture frequently as it cooks, about 10 minutes. When mixture is thickened and lines remain in the mixture when the whisk is lifted, add the cubed butter. Continue to whisk over medium heat until the butter is incorporated and the mixture is smooth.

3. Remove from heat and strain through a fine mesh sieve. Cover by setting plastic wrap directly on the surface of the lemon curd; chill for 20 minutes.

4. Preheat oven to 350°F. Use a 2 1/2-inch round cutter to cut 18 circles from the pound cake. Place 6 circles on a serving platter; put 1 1/2 tablespoons of lemon curd on top of the cake circles. Top with raspberries. Top each with another cake circle, 1 1/2 tablespoons of lemon curd, and more raspberries.

5. Place remaining 6 cake circles on a baking sheet; set aside. In a stainless steel mixing bowl or double boiler combine the remaining 1 cup sugar and the egg whites. Put the bowl or double boiler over a saucepan of simmering water; whisk until egg white mixture is warm to the touch. Remove from heat. With an electric mixer whip the mixture on high until the mixture holds soft peaks.

6. Put the whipped whites in a piping bag with a plain tip. Pipe designs on top of the remaining cake circles. Bake 10 minutes or until meringue is golden. Top each dessert with a meringue layer and serve.

# apple tart with caramel sauce and vanilla ice cream

makes 4 servings

- 1/2 of a 17.3-ounce package frozen puff pastry sheets
- 3 small Granny Smith apples
- 1/4 cup sugar
- 1/4 teaspoon ground cinnamon
- 1 to 2 tablespoons butter, cut into small pieces
- Caramel Sauce (see recipe, below)
- Vanilla ice cream

CARAMEL SAUCE

- 1 1/2 cups sugar
- 1/4 cup water
- 1 cup whipping cream
- 1 tablespoon unsalted butter

1. Preheat oven to 375°F. On a lightly floured surface cut out four 4-inch circles from sheet of puff pastry. Place rounds on a parchment-lined baking sheet.

2. Peel and core the apples. Cut each apple in half. Thinly slice apples. Arrange the apple slices in a circle on top of each pastry round so they overlap slightly. In a small bowl combine the sugar and cinnamon and sprinkle on top of the apples. Top each tart with some butter.

3. Bake for 25 minutes or until the pastry is golden and the apples are tender. Serve with Caramel Sauce and vanilla ice cream.

CARAMEL SAUCE

1. In a large saucepan combine sugar and water. Cook and stir over high heat until sugar is dissolved and mixture comes to a boil.

2. Reduce heat to medium. Continue cooking, stirring occasionally, until the mixture is a golden color.

3. Remove from heat. Carefully whisk in cream, half at a time. Stir in butter. Return to medium heat to melt any sugar lumps. Let cool.

# carrot cake with cream cheese frosting

makes 16 servings

- 1 1/2 cups all-purpose flour
- 1 1/2 cups granulated sugar
- 1/2 teaspoon salt
- 1/2 teaspoon baking soda
- 1/2 teaspoon ground cinnamon
- 3/4 cup vegetable oil
- 2 eggs
- 1 1/2 teaspoons vanilla
- 3/4 cup finely shredded carrots
- 3/4 cup chopped walnuts
- 3/4 cup shredded coconut
- 1/2 of an 8-ounce can pineapple chunks, drained
- 1 8-ounce package cream cheese, softened
- 1/2 cup unsalted butter, softened
- 5 1/2 to 6 cups powdered sugar

1. Preheat oven to 325°F. Grease a 9-inch Bundt® pan and set aside. In a large bowl combine the flour, the granulated sugar, the salt, baking soda, and cinnamon. Mix well. In a medium bowl whisk together the oil, eggs, and 1/2 teaspoon of the vanilla. Mix egg mixture into the flour mixture. Fold in the carrots, walnuts, coconut, and pineapple until combined.

2. Pour batter into the prepared cake pan; bake for 45 minutes or until a toothpick inserted in the center comes out clean. Cool in the pan 15 minutes. Invert cake onto a wire rack and cool completely.

3. Meanwhile, for the frosting, in large mixing bowl beat the cream cheese and butter with an electric mixer on medium speed. Beat in the remaining 1 teaspoon vanilla. Slowly add the powdered sugar, scraping bowl between additions of powdered sugar. Continue mixing until smooth. Chill in the refrigerator until of spreading consistency. Spread the cream cheese frosting over the cooled cake.

# jack and cake

makes 16 servings

- 2 tablespoons unsalted butter, melted
- 1 pound unsalted butter, softened
- 2½ cups sugar
- 9 egg yolks
- 4¾ cups cake flour
- 4 teaspoons baking powder
- 1¾ cups Jack Daniels® Tennessee whiskey
- 9 egg whites

1. Preheat oven to 350°F. Brush the inside of a 9-inch Bundt® pan with the 2 tablespoons melted butter. In a large mixing bowl beat the 1 pound butter with an electric mixer on medium speed for 30 seconds. Add 1¼ cups of the sugar and continue to cream the mixture until fluffy. Add the egg yolks one at a time. Turn to low speed and slowly add the flour and baking powder until combined, scraping down sides of the bowl as necessary. Add ¼ cup of the whiskey and beat until combined; set aside

2. Put the egg whites in a clean mixing bowl. Beat with an electric mixer on high speed until soft peaks form. Gradually add the remaining 1¼ cups sugar until combined. Fold the egg white mixture into the cake batter. Pour the batter into the prepared pan.

3. Bake for 1 hour or until the cake is golden and a toothpick inserted into the center comes out clean. Cool in the pan on a wire rack for 15 minutes. Pour ¾ cup of the whiskey over the cake. Put a plate on top of the cake, flip over, and remove the cake pan. Pour the remaining ¾ cup of whiskey over the cake. Slice and serve.

"YES. YES. IF YOU'VE EVER WANTED JACK AS A FRIEND, NOW YOU HAVE A REASON TO HAVE JACK AS YOUR FRIEND."

# dark chocolate mousse

makes 6 servings

- 1/2 cup milk
- 2 cups whipping cream
- 4 egg yolks
- 1/2 cup sugar
- 1 tablespoon vanilla
- 10 ounces dark chocolate, chopped
- Sweetened whipped cream
- Shaved dark chocolate
- Fresh raspberries

1. In a small saucepan combine the milk and 1/2 cup of the cream. Bring to boiling on high heat.

2. In a large bowl whisk together the egg yolks and sugar until well combined. Whisk a small amount of the milk mixture into the yolk mixture. Gradually whisk in remaining milk mixture. Add the vanilla and continue whisking until well combined. Strain the mixture through a fine mesh sieve.

3. While still hot, pour the mixture over the chopped chocolate. Let stand for 5 minutes. Whisk mixture until smooth. Set aside and let cool.

4. Whip the remaining 1 1/2 cups cream until soft peaks form. When the chocolate mixture is no longer warm to the touch, stir a small amount of whipped cream into the chocolate mixture to lighten. Fold in remaining whipped cream.

5. Scoop the chocolate mousse into six chilled 6-ounce glasses. Set in the fridge for at least 1 hour. Top with additional sweetened whipped cream, shaved chocolate, and fresh raspberries.

# dark chocolate flourless cake

makes 8 to 10 servings

- 10 ounces dark chocolate, chopped
- 10 tablespoons unsalted butter
- 7 egg yolks
- Unsweetened cocoa powder
- Fresh berries
- Fresh mint leaves

1. Preheat oven to 350°F. Grease an 8-inch cake pan and line the bottom of the pan with parchment paper; set aside.

2. Combine the chocolate and the butter in a stainless steel bowl or double boiler. Place the bowl over, but not touching, a pan of simmering water to melt the butter and chocolate, mixing with a rubber spatula to make sure there are no lumps. Remove the chocolate mixture from the heat.

3. In a large mixing bowl beat egg yolks with an electric mixer on high speed until they triple in volume. Carefully fold the beaten egg yolks into the chocolate mixture.

4. Pour the batter into the prepared cake pan. Put the cake pan in a roasting pan. Put the roasting pan on a baking rack in the oven. Pour enough boiling water into the roasting pan to reach halfway up the sides of the cake pan. Bake for 25 to 30 minutes. Remove from the oven and keep in the water for another 5 minutes. Remove cake pan from the roasting pan.

5. Chill cake in refrigerator for 2 to 3 hours. Put a plate over cake pan and invert to remove cake. Put another plate on the bottom of the cake and flip again to get it right-side up. Sprinkle cake with cocoa powder; top with fresh berries and mint leaves.

# caramel pot de crème

makes 6 servings

- 2 cups sugar
- 1/2 cup water
- 4 cups whipping cream
- 2 cups milk
- 12 egg yolks
- Sweetened whipped cream or frozen whipped dessert topping, thawed

1. Preheat oven to 325°F. In a large saucepan combine the sugar and water. Mix with a spoon just to make sure there are no pockets of dry sugar. Bring to boiling over high heat. Reduce heat and, without stirring, continue cooking until mixture reaches the desired caramel color.

2. Remove from heat and carefully whisk in 1 cup of the cream. Gradually stir in remaining 3 cups cream and the milk. Return to medium heat and cook, stirring, to smooth out any sugar lumps.

3. Remove from heat and cool for 10 minutes.

4. In a large bowl whisk the yolks. Whisk about a cup of the caramel mixture into the yolks. Slowly whisk in the remaining caramel mixture. Strain mixture through a fine-mesh sieve.

5. Pour mixture into six 8-ounce ramekins and place in a large baking dish or roasting pan. Add enough boiling water to come halfway up the sides of the ramekins. Cover ramekins with foil. Bake about 1 hour or until the center jiggles only slightly when you tap the side of the pan. Remove from the oven and let stand in the hot water for another 5 minutes.

6. Remove ramekins from the baking dish and chill in the refrigerator for at least 20 minutes before serving. Top with sweetened whipped cream and serve.

# double chocolate blondies

makes 36 servings

- 18 ounces white chocolate, chopped
- 4 tablespoons unsalted butter
- 1/2 cup water
- 1/2 cup sugar
- 4 eggs
- 1 1/2 cups all-purpose flour
- 1 teaspoon salt
- 1 1/2 cups macadamia nuts, chopped

1. Preheat oven to 350°F. Line a 15×10×1-inch baking pan with parchment paper; set aside. In a stainless steel bowl or double boiler combine half (9 ounces) of the chocolate, the butter, water, and sugar. Place over, but not touching, a saucepan of simmering water on low heat, stirring until melted.

2. In a large bowl whisk the eggs. Whisk in a small amount of the chocolate mixture. Gradually whisk in remaining chocolate mixture. Add the flour and salt and continue whisking until well combined. Fold in the remaining 9 ounces chopped chocolate and the nuts.

3. Pour into prepared pan. Bake for 20 to 25 minutes or until small cracks appear on the edges. Cool on a wire rack for 20 minutes before serving.

# double chocolate brownies

makes 36 servings

- 18 ounces dark chocolate, chopped
- 4 tablespoons unsalted butter
- ½ cup water
- ½ cup sugar
- 4 whole eggs
- 1½ cups all-purpose flour
- 1 teaspoon salt
- 1½ cups walnuts, chopped

1. Preheat oven to 350°F. Line a 15×10×1-inch baking pan with parchment paper; set aside. In a stainless steel bowl or double boiler combine half (9 ounces) of the chocolate, the butter, water, and sugar. Place over, but not touching, a saucepan of simmering water on low heat, stirring until melted.

2. In a large bowl lightly beat the eggs. Whisk in a small amount of the chocolate mixture. Gradually whisk in remaining chocolate mixture. Add the flour and salt and continue whisking until well combined. Fold in the remaining 9 ounces chopped chocolate and the nuts.

3. Pour into prepared pan. Bake for 20 to 25 minutes or until small cracks appear on the edges. Cool on a wire rack for 20 minutes before serving.

“THIS IS YOUR MAKE-UP DESSERT ... LONG NIGHT ... NOW THINGS ARE OK. LET'S GET TO THE DOUBLE CHOCOLATE BROWNIES!”

# 9 FAMILY AND FRIENDS

growing up, everyone in my family learned to cook together. We watched in secret to see whose dish went over better at big meals and we tasted each others' recipes on the side to see for ourselves. The competition today is much the same with friends who have their own successful careers but still like to cook—like my man Dennis (aka Big Den), who is a partner in a big law firm and swears his version of his grandma's peach cobbler is the best dessert ever. That's what this chapter is all about: getting together and bringing both good food and some friendly competition to the table!

# shrimp and chicken alfredo with noodles —patrick wright

makes 4 to 6 servings

1 12-ounce package dried no yolk noodles
1 to 2 skinless, boneless chicken breast halves
1 tablespoon cooking oil
1 17-ounce jar Alfredo pasta sauce
½ cup white wine
¼ cup sliced green onions
1 pound medium shrimp, peeled and deveined
Salt and ground black pepper

1. Cook noodles according to package directions.

2. Cut chicken into thin strips. In a large sauté pan heat oil over medium heat. Add chicken and cook until no longer pink.

3. Stir in Alfredo sauce, wine, and green onions. Bring to boiling. Add shrimp and cook 3 minutes more or until shrimp is opaque. Stir in noodles. Season to taste with salt and black pepper. Serve immediately.

# brother-in-law barbecue ribs —kevin veasey

makes 6 to 8 servings

- 2 slabs of pork loin back (baby back) ribs
- 1 23-ounce bottle La Lechonera Mojo Criollo Spanish Marinating Sauce (or see Mojo Sauce recipe, below)

1. Place ribs in a very large resealable bag set in a shallow pan. Add mojo sauce. Seal bag. Marinate overnight, turning occasionally.

2. Remove ribs from marinade, discarding marinade. Arrange medium-hot coals around a drip pan. Test for medium heat above the pan. Place ribs, bone side down, on the grill rack over the drip pan. Cover and grill 1½ to 1¾ hours or until tender.

MOJO SAUCE
In a small bowl combine ½ cup orange juice, ½ cup olive oil, ¼ cup G's Blackening Spice, and 8 cloves garlic, minced.

# spaghetti —eleanor beasley

makes 4 to 6 servings

- 1 pound ground beef or uncooked ground turkey
- 1 medium onion, chopped
- 2 celery stalks, chopped (optional)
- 2½ cups water
- ⅔ cup ketchup
- 1 6-ounce can tomato paste
- 1 tablespoon dried oregano
- 1 tablespoon Italian seasoning
- Dash ground allspice
- 1 16-ounce package dried spaghetti pasta

1. In a Dutch oven brown ground beef, onion, and celery, if using. Drain fat.

2. Add water, ketchup, tomato paste, oregano, Italian seasoning, and allspice to ground beef mixture. Bring to boiling. Reduce heat and simmer, uncovered, for 45 minutes.

3. Meanwhile cook pasta according to package directions. Drain and add to sauce.

# sue's shrimp and pasta salad —renita "sue" veasey

makes 8 to 10 servings

- 1 pound dried spaghetti pasta
- 1 pound medium shrimp, peeled and deveined
- 1 green bell pepper, chopped
- 1 red bell pepper, chopped
- 1 yellow bell pepper, chopped
- 1/2 cup chopped onion
- 1 16-ounce bottle Italian salad dressing
- 1 tablespoon Salad Supreme® seasoning

1. Cook spaghetti according to package directions, adding shrimp the last 3 minutes of cooking time. Drain. Run cold water over the pasta and shrimp to cool; drain again.

2. In a large bowl combine pasta, shrimp, all the peppers, and onion. Add salad dressing and salad seasoning. Mix well and chill for 30 minutes before serving.

# squash casserole —carla wright

makes 6 to 8 servings

- 1 0.4-ounce packet dry ranch salad dressing mix
- 1 egg, lightly beaten
- 8 ounces shredded cheddar cheese (2 cups)
- 6 to 8 yellow summer squash, cut in 1/4-inch slices
- 1 medium onion, chopped
- Salt and ground black pepper
- 6 to 8 saltine crackers, coarsely broken

1. Preheat oven to 350°F. In a large bowl prepare salad dressing according to package directions. Add egg and 1½ cups of the cheese. Add squash and onion. Sprinkle with salt and pepper and toss to coat

2. Transfer squash mixture to a 2-quart greased baking dish. Top with remaining ½ cup cheese and the saltine crackers. Bake 30 minutes or until squash is tender.

# vegetable medley –my mom

makes 4 to 6 servings

- 1 tablespoon unsalted butter
- 4 cloves garlic, chopped
- 1 small onion, sliced
- 2 yellow squash, sliced
- 1/2 head broccoli florets
- 1/2 head cauliflower florets
- 1/2 pint mushrooms, sliced
- 3 plum tomatoes, diced
- 1/4 cup water
- 1/2 cube chicken bouillon
- Salt and black pepper

1. In a large sauté pan melt butter over medium heat. Add garlic; sauté for 2 to 3 minutes or until garlic starts to turn brown. Add onion and cook for 3 minutes.

2. Add yellow squash, broccoli, cauliflower, mushrooms, and tomatoes. Cook and stir for 3 minutes more. Stir in water, bouillon, and salt and pepper to taste. Simmer until bouillon is dissolved and vegetables are tender.

# cheesecake —patrick wright

makes 16 servings

- 2 8-ounce packages cream cheese
- 1 14-ounce can sweetened condensed milk
- 2 egg yolks
- 1 teaspoon vanilla
- 2 9-inch graham cracker crumb pie shells

1. Preheat oven to 350°F. In a large mixing bowl beat cream cheese with an electric mixer until smooth with no lumps. Add sweetened condensed milk, egg yolks, and vanilla. Mix well and pour into pie shells.

2. Bake for 20 minutes or until center is nearly set. Cool to room temperature then chill at least 4 hours before serving.

# peach cobbler —dennis ellis (aka big den)

makes 6 to 8 servings

- 1 recipe Crust (see recipe, below)
- 2 16-ounce packages frozen peach slices
- 1½ cups sugar
- 1 cup water
- 2 tablespoons all-purpose flour
- 1½ teaspoons ground nutmeg
- ¼ cup chilled butter, cut into small pieces
- Sugar
- Ground nutmeg
- Vanilla ice cream (optional)

1. Preheat oven to 350°F. Prepare the Crust. For the filling, in a large bowl combine the peaches, the 1½ cups sugar, and the water; mix well. Then add the flour and the 1½ teaspoons nutmeg; mix together.

2. Divide the crust into two balls, one slightly larger than the other. On a floured surface, roll the small ball of crust out to fit the bottom of an 11×9×2-inch baking dish. Put the crust in the bottom of the dish. Spoon the peach filling mixture into the pastry in the dish. Roll out the larger ball of crust to fit over the top. Put the top on, pinching the edges to seal as well as possible. Dot the crust with ¼ cup butter; sprinkle with additional sugar and nutmeg.

3. Bake about 1 hour, or until crust is brown and filling has thickened. Let cool about 30 minutes before serving. Serve with ice cream, if desired.

CRUST

- 2 cups all-purpose flour
- 1 tablespoon sugar
- ½ teaspoon baking powder
- ½ teaspoon salt
- 1¼ cups chilled butter, cut into small pieces
- 4 to 5 tablespoons milk

CRUST

1. In a large bowl combine flour, sugar, baking powder, and salt.

2. Using a pastry blender, cut in butter until the pieces are pea-size. Sprinkle 1 tablespoon of the milk over the flour mixture; toss with a fork. Repeat with remaining milk until all the flour mixture is moistened. Form into a ball with your hands. Add more milk as needed. If it gets too wet add a little more flour to even it out.

**ingredients** Be adventurous and try ingredients you might not have cooked with before. If you're not sure what to buy, here's what to watch for. And because a few of these items go by different names, let's get that cleared up while we're at it.

## HERBS

1. ITALIAN OR FLAT-LEAF PARSLEY
2. THYME
3. BASIL
4. ROSEMARY—LIKE THYME, YOU CAN USE IT ALL OR STRIP AND CHOP THE LEAVES.
5. CILANTRO

## MUSHROOMS

1. SHIITAKE—BECAUSE THEY ARE VERSATILE AND WIDELY AVAILABLE.

2. OYSTER—AMAZING DELICATE TEXTURE IS THE PULL HERE.

3. TRUMPET, ALSO CALLED KING TRUMPET—THIS IS ONE INSANELY MEATY MUSHROOM.

## LETTUCE

1. & 3. ARUGULA—SPICY AND PUNGENT; ALSO KNOWN AS EITHER ROCKET OR ROQUETTE.

2. BUTTERHEAD LETTUCE— MILD, TENDER, SWEET. IT ALSO GOES BY BUTTER LEAF, BIBB, AND BOSTON.

4. FRISÉE, ALSO SOMETIMES CALLED CURLY ENDIVE.

2
3

# BREADS

THE BEST WAY TO LIVEN UP SANDWICHES IS TO GET CREATIVE WITH THE BREAD. I CALL FOR ALL OF THESE IN THE RECIPES, BUT MAKE SURE YOU EXPERIMENT WITH THEM ON YOUR OWN TOO.

1. BAGUETTE
2. CIABATTA
3. FOCACCIA
4. HOAGIE
5. SOURDOUGH

## PANCETTA /PROSCIUTTO

1. PANCETTA—ITALIAN-STYLE, DRY-CURED, ROLLED BACON THAT IS NEVER SMOKED.

2. PROSCIUTTO—A DRY-CURED ITALIAN HAM, SLICED PAPER THIN, ALSO NOT SMOKED. DON'T SUB PANCETTA FOR PROSCIUTTO OR VICE VERSA. I INSTEAD USE DRY-CURED BACON FOR PANCETTA AND DRY-CURED HAM FOR PROSCIUTTO.

## GREEN MUSSELS / CALAMARI / BLACK MUSSELS

BUY ANY OF THESE FRESH OR FROZEN:

1. GREEN-LIPPED, OR NEW ZEALAND GREEN MUSSELS

2. CALAMARI—IF FRESH, ASK THE FISHMONGER TO CLEAN IT FOR YOU.

3. BLACK MUSSELS—GOOD SUB FOR GREEN MUSSELS ANYTIME.

BY THE WAY, FROZEN VERSIONS OF ALL OF THESE USUALLY COME PRE-CLEANED.

## SEAFOOD

1. ATLANTIC SALMON
2. RED SNAPPER—ASK TO HAVE IT CLEANED, IF WHOLE.
3. SWORDFISH
4. AHI TUNA
5. CHILEAN SEA BASS
6. SKATE—ALSO CALLED SKATE WING.

REMEMBER, IT'S OK TO ASK TO SMELL SEAFOOD BEFORE YOU BUY. IF IT DOESN'T SMELL CLEAN AND FRESH, DON'T BUY IT.

“WITH A SMALL AMOUNT OF TRUST IN YOURSELF AND THE SUPPORT OF GOOD FRIENDS, YOU CAN COOK AND ENJOY INCREDIBLE MEALS IN THE COMFORT OF YOUR OWN HOME.

—G”

**final thoughts** In recent months I've been on the road doing cooking demos, book signings, and guest appearances. I hit Charlotte, then Ohio, New Orleans, San Francisco, Orlando, New York (for another *Good Morning America* spot), Des Moines, and Charleston in just a matter of days. With a life and schedule like this, I absolutely must find the greater good in all things. The one thing that I know to be true about all this travel and all the great shows and great people that I'm fortunate to meet is that every town has a few people who have decided for one day that they're not going to go out to some fancy restaurant or hotel. Instead they're going to go to the market and get some fresh produce and have the butcher hand-prepare some great cuts of meat. Then they'll run by the wine store, read a few labels, and taste something new from, say, South Africa. I can only imagine they'll also stop for some amazing cheese, a little caviar, and finally fresh flowers for the dining room table. Sounds like a wonderful home-cooked meal is on the horizon.

While I haven't been lucky enough to be invited to anyone's home for one of these meals while I'm traveling, I am certain that they do exist. (Now, if you want to invite me over next time I'm in town ...)

Putting together a special meal allows you to explore your creative chromosomes, to create something that you'll probably discover isn't at all difficult. With a small amount of trust in yourself and the support of good friends, you can cook and enjoy restaurant-worthy meals in the comfort of your own home.

Please take the recipes from this book and have some fun at home with your family and friends.
I look forward to hearing your stories while you dine in.

Peace,
G. Garvin

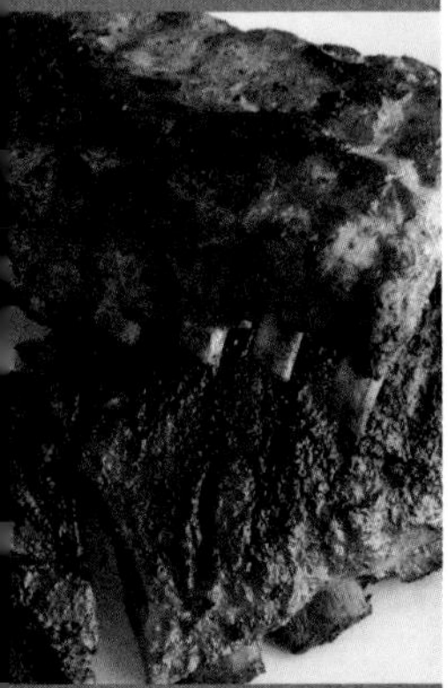

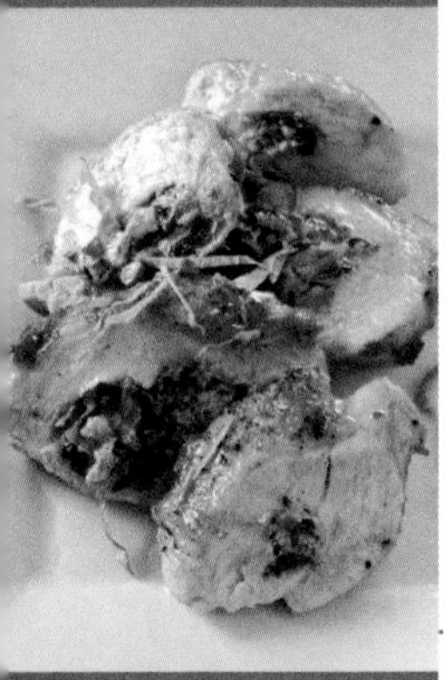

# index

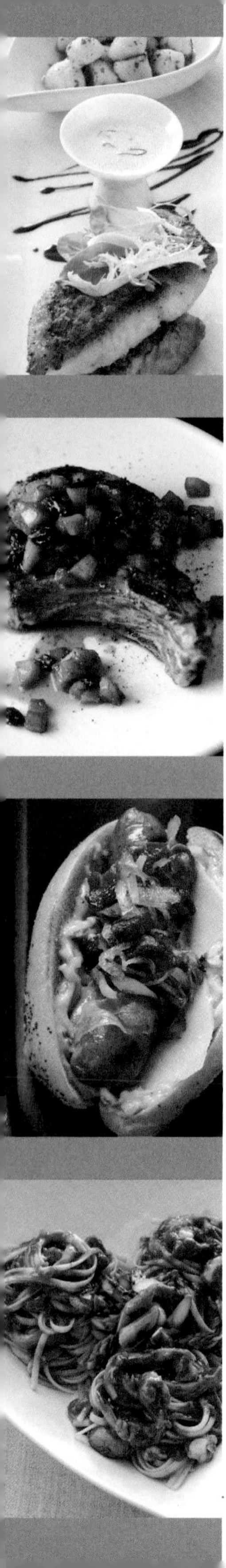

G. GARVIN'S
TURN UP THE HEAT &
THE ROAD TOUR
Make it super simple!
Saturdays on
tv One
www.tvoneonline.com